Gender Dive
and Inclusic
Early Years Education

CH00730526

How can we support children to reach their full potential and not be constrained by gender expectations? Are gender roles fixed at birth or do they develop through experiences? *Gender Diversity and Inclusion in Early Years Education* introduces practitioners to key aspects of gender in the early years and explores how to ensure that children and staff teams are supported in settings that have outstanding practice.

Considering the implications of gender in the context of supporting children, families and practitioners, this book examines the theoretical contexts that surround gender identity and explores current legislation and practice in order to provide practitioners with all the information they need to develop their own work and settings in an open and equal way. Offering a wealth of practical guidance, case studies and reflective questions which link to the EYFS, chapters cover:

- a theoretical approach to gender development;

- current legislation and the impact on early years practice;

- understanding gender fluidity and the way in which children express gender;

- creating gender equality when working with children and the role of the manager in creating a supportive ethos.

Including tasks, reflective points and links to useful websites and organisations, this book will be valuable reading for all early years practitioners and students who want to promote an inclusive environment for the children in their care, their families and colleagues.

Kath Tayler is a Senior Lecturer in Early Years Education at the University of Brighton, UK. She has worked in early years for over 30 years as a nursery nurse, primary teacher and lecturer in early years education and care in both further and higher education.

Deborah Price is a Senior Lecturer at the University of Brighton and an Associate Lecturer at The Open University, UK. She has worked in early and primary years as a teacher, trainer, inspector and lecturer.

Diversity and Inclusion in the Early Years

Gender Diversity and Inclusion in Early Years Education
Kath Tayler and Deborah Price

LGBT Diversity and Inclusion in Early Years Education
Deborah Price and Kath Tayler

Gender Diversity and Inclusion in Early Years Education

Kath Tayler and Deborah Price

Routledge
Taylor & Francis Group

LONDON AND NEW YORK

First published 2016
by Routledge
2 Park Square, Milton Park, Abingdon, Oxon OX14 4RN

and by Routledge
711 Third Avenue, New York, NY 10017

Routledge is an imprint of the Taylor & Francis Group, an informa business

© 2016 Kath Tayler and Deborah Price

The right of Kath Tayler and Deborah Price to be identified as authors of this work has been asserted by them in accordance with sections 77 and 78 of the Copyright, Designs and Patents Act 1988.

All rights reserved. No part of this book may be reprinted or reproduced or utilised in any form or by any electronic, mechanical, or other means, now known or hereafter invented, including photocopying and recording, or in any information storage or retrieval system, without permission in writing from the publishers.

Trademark notice: Product or corporate names may be trademarks or registered trademarks, and are used only for identification and explanation without intent to infringe.

British Library Cataloguing in Publication Data
A catalogue record for this book is available from the British Library

Library of Congress Cataloging-in-Publication Data
Names: Tayler, Kath, author. | Price, Deborah, author.
Title: Gender diversity and inclusion in early years education / Kath Tayler and Deborah Price.
Description: New York, NY : Routledge, 2016.
Identifiers: LCCN 2015042072| ISBN 9781138857100 (hardback) |
ISBN 9781138857117 (pbk.) | ISBN 9781315718903 (ebook)
Subjects: LCSH: Sex differences in education. | Gender identity in education.
| Early childhood education—Social aspects.
Classification: LCC LC212.9 .T38 2016 | DDC 372.21—dc23
LC record available at http://lccn.loc.gov/2015042072

ISBN: 978-1-138-85710-0 (hbk)
ISBN: 978-1-138-85711-7 (pbk)
ISBN: 978-1-315-71890-3 (ebk)

Typeset in Optima
by Keystroke, Station Road, Codsall, Wolverhampton

Printed and bound in Great Britain
by Ashford Colour Press Ltd, Gosport, Hampshire

Dedication

Kath Tayler: To Morwenna, Jocelyn and Emmeline with love always.

Deborah Price: I dedicate this book with love to my brother Danny Lubert.

Contents

Acknowledgements

Central to this book, particularly the case studies, are all the children, families, practitioners and students we have worked with over many years. We are enormously grateful to them for sharing their stories.

Additional grateful thanks to the staff of One World Nursery in Brighton who were so generous with their time and their ideas. Thanks also to Fen Coles from Letterbox Library who has supported and advised us throughout. Similarly, thanks to Clair Barnard from the Early Childhood Project, Brighton. Thanks also to colleagues in the University of Brighton who have been supportive and helpful with our research and writing. We would like to thank Stephanie Thornton for the generous sharing of her experiences and Dr Cathy Ota for the use of 'Menu for Change', inspired from Working with Others training (www. workingwithothers.org).

Special thanks to Marijke Acket and Maria Jastrzebska for their thoughtful input.

1   **Introduction**

As an early years practitioner you may have chosen to read this book because you are interested in gender in the early years and thinking about how gender impacts on the children you work with. You may be asking yourself the following questions. What does it mean to be a girl or a boy? Are boys and girls born different or does society shape our expectations and our behaviour? Is there just one way to be a girl and one way to be a boy or are there many ways of expressing gender? How do childhood expressions of gender influence the way children grow up into women and men? Do we hold the same views about gender as we did 50 years ago? What has caused the changes that have taken place?

As well as encouraging you to think about these practical questions and to consider possible causes, this book provides you with some theoretical underpinning to enable you to set the issues in a context and to support you as you reflect on your practice. We examine questions that have challenged early years practitioners and provide you with opportunities to think reflectively about gender in relation to your practice. The case studies and discussions will provide you with ways forward and will support you as you think about any actions or changes you want to implement. This will enable you to work towards achieving outstanding practice in terms of gender diversity and to take account of any statutory responsibilities you have.

There are significant and ongoing changes currently taking place within early childhood provision in the UK and it is therefore critical to reflect on how gender equity within the early years phase is likely to be promoted by central government initiatives and the developments being introduced by early years educators.

(Browne 2004: 1)

Consider the following comments about gender made by early years practitioners.

- I was on holiday recently and in the hotel they gave all the children activity packs when they arrived. The girls got bright pink princess packs and the boys got blue and black pirate packs. The little girl of the family in front of us didn't seem at all interested in her pack and enviously eyed her brother's pirate pack. Why couldn't they just hold out both packs and let the children choose?

- When the children in our setting have a new baby in the family, we like to send the family a card. We decided we wanted to try to send ones that were gender neutral. This is really difficult! All the cards are pink or blue and refer to the new baby girl or boy. In the end we made our own cards by scanning and printing pictures the children had painted.

- When you work in a baby room you can really see that they are different from birth. Boys and girls just behave differently even from that early age. We don't treat them any different but they are different so it must be biology.

- Most of the parents in our setting have expectations about how their sons and daughters will behave. They generally dress them according to whether they are boys or girls and buy them toys according to that too. It is quite unusual to have a parent who wants their child to be different in that respect.

- All children should be given opportunities to explore all types of play. We try to avoid stereotyping the activities that might be of interest to boys and girls.

All these examples show that early years practitioners are aware of the gender differences of the children in their settings and in wider society. They also show that there is an ongoing debate about whether the differences we see between boys and girls are innate or socially constructed. This nature/nurture debate remains unanswered and possibly unanswerable. While many studies have claimed to scientifically prove that there are biological differences that account for behavioural differences, many of these studies have been critiqued and their methodology found wanting (for a very clear account of some of the research in this area see Fine 2011).

From the perspective of the many early years practitioners who are interested in and questioning about gender differences in early childhood, there may be a twofold aspect to this interest. Firstly it may be of interest to try to understand where these differences come from.

I've worked with young children for many years and I have always felt that the general differences I encounter between boys and girls are innate. I have observed many differences even in babies. Baby boys seem to be more active and physical in their play while baby girls seem more passive. However, I then saw something on television where they did an experiment with babies. They put a baby in a blue Babygro and instructed adults to play with the baby. They then put the same baby in a pink Babygro and gave adults the same instructions. They filmed the interactions and analysed them. They found there were subtle differences in how the adults behaved depending on whether they assumed the baby was a boy or a girl. They were more physical with the 'boy' and bounced the baby around. With the 'girl' they were more gentle and soothing. This made me think about how we treat the babies in my setting and that maybe it isn't all biological!

(early years practitioner)

Secondly, practitioners may be particularly interested in thinking about what we do about gender differences in our daily interactions with babies and young children. Are there changes that can be made to provision? What challenges are there in terms of activities? How can practitioners interact with the children they work with to challenge stereotyping? How can parents be involved in these challenges? How can teams of practitioners work together to develop best practice in this area? What are the implications of having an almost entirely female workforce?

> I've recently started working in an early years setting after working with older children. The other day I caught myself asking for some 'big, strong boys' to help put the bikes away! When I thought about this I realised that I often compliment the girls for how pretty they look as well. I don't know where this came from as I would think of myself as committed to giving all the girls and boys an equal experience in the setting. I started to think about what practical changes I need to make to my practice in order to be fully inclusive and one thing I did straight away was to compliment all the children on their achievements rather than how they looked.
>
> (early years practitioner)

As Brown reminds us, 'while learning about the world around them children pick up both positive and negative attitudes and behaviour' (2007: 11). They can learn that boys and girls have choices and that they can all be strong, caring, gentle and powerful or they can learn that boys have more power than girls but that they don't cry and can't be caring. All those working in the early years have a responsibility to provide children with opportunities and experiences that encourage the full range of human emotions and capacities.

At the same time it is crucial to understand that children have agency and power. They are not blank slates waiting to have the norms of any given culture inscribed upon them. They will develop their own ways of thinking about gender and their own understandings of our gendered world (Kane 2013).

How to use this book

This is unlikely to be a book that you read from beginning to end. It is a book to dip into, a resource for you to use and a starting point for discussions and staff training. The case studies and activities will provide you with lots to think about and may lead you to think about your own practice in different ways. This can be challenging but can lead to a team who value the contribution you each have to make and will support you as you think about issues to do with gender and identity. Crucial to this will be the support from the manager who has the role of developing the ethos of the setting and of creating an enabling environment, not just for the children but for the practitioners and parents as well.

The chapters can be read independently of each other and don't need to be read in order although we do suggest you start with Chapter 2. When you come to activities and case studies we suggest that you read it through and use the *points for discussion* to guide the way you discuss the issue within your team. You might like to save the *discussion* and read this after your own discussion as this may enable you to come up with the ideas most relevant to your own setting and your practice rather than be guided by our ideas.

Chapter breakdown

Chapter 2 – What's it all about?

This chapter lays out the main theoretical views about how gender identity develops and it is probably a good idea to start with this as it informs the discussions in the rest of the book. A case study of a group of children playing together weaves through the chapter to help you to think about the ideas being discussed.

You are encouraged to think beyond providing developmentally appropriate practice in order to consider what meanings children might be building about gender. Biological and socialisation theories are considered before moving on to look at the child's own agency and power in challenging gendered behaviour. You will also be introduced to some of the terms you will encounter throughout the book.

Chapter 3 – Legislative background

Legislation has a direct impact on practice and so this chapter helps you to think about the relevant policy and legislation. The chapter starts with a look at the historical progression of legislation in relation to gender and the impact this has had on the lives of groups and individuals.

Current legislation that impacts on early years practice is then considered in terms of the responsibility towards children in the setting and the employees in the setting. This section includes a discussion about the four nation states and how England, Scotland, Northern Ireland and Wales work towards gender equality in their early years documents.

Chapter 4 – Working with families

This chapter looks at how we understand gender fluidity and considers the way in which children express gender. We explore the idea that this can change and vary over time. This is put in the context of how the arrangement of clothes, toys, etc. into separate categories for boys and girls can limit and define their choices.

These issues are highlighted with a case study of a transgender child and the way in which the setting supported the child and the family and a further case study looking at how a setting supported a family with a transgender parent. While these situations may be unusual, this chapter encourages you to think about the gender fluidity of all children.

Chapter 5 – Working with children

This chapter asks if we should make all activities available to all children in the hope we will create gender equality or if we need to be more proactive in how we approach this. This is largely explored through a case study based on an interview with practitioners at One World Nursery in Brighton. By looking at some action research they carried out about superhero play, their commitment to challenging gender inequality is explored.

The chapter also encourages you to 'think outside the box' when observing children's behaviour and uses schema theory as an example of other ways in which children's play may be understood.

Chapter 6 – Leading and managing good practice

The role of the manager in creating a supportive ethos is explored in this chapter. This is considered in terms of developing a clear and inclusive vision statement. Guidance is also given on how vision statements could be used.

Alongside this, the role of men in early years is considered. Their role is explored in terms of the role models they can provide and the challenge this presents to traditional male and female roles in early years settings. The issue of safeguarding is then considered, particularly in relation to assumptions around men who wish to work with young children.

Chapter 7 – Resources

While acknowledging the importance of the many excellent resources available for young children, this chapter encourages you to think of the adults in a setting as one of the main resources. The interactions you have and the way you support children will be of significant importance in terms of their developing understandings about gender.

The way in which you support children engaging with books, imaginative play, dressing-up and small world toys is discussed as well as encouraging you to think about the messages conveyed through your displays.

Chapter 8 – Conclusion

In the concluding chapter of the book we draw together the ideas and discussions from the previous chapters. We provide some thoughts from children about gender and ask you to discuss them using your ideas developed through reading the book.

The key themes of the book are then summarised followed by a 'menu' of different things you could implement in your setting. The book ends with a short summary of the main underpinning ideas that we should all be aiming for; to move thinking and practice forward in order to provide the best possible environment for our youngest children.

Finally

This book will hopefully encourage you to look at the children in your setting with fresh eyes. The activities and case studies will ask you to look beyond any assumptions you may have about gender and how children develop their gender identity. You need to be willing to think beyond the idea that boys and girls are born different or the idea that they simply learn to be different in their families and their communities. While acknowledging the importance of biology and society, you need to be open to exploring children's own agency and ability to be meaning makers.

Asking yourself searching questions will help you think deeply about gender and enable you to make the most of this book.

- What sense does this child make of this activity? In what ways does their gender influence their reaction to the activity?

- In what way does this child understand this story? Do they see reflections of themselves in it and does it provide role models of a range of ways of being male or female?

- How has this child decided to play in this way? Are they given choices and support for playing in a range of ways?

- How am I interpreting this? Is there another way? What impact does my own history in terms of gender have on how I view children?

- Am I making assumptions about this child's play because s/he is a girl/boy? What can I do to challenge these assumptions and how can I get support with that?

Being open and honest with yourself, your colleagues, parents and children will enable you to make the most of the activities and ideas you will find as you read. Above all, we hope you enjoy this book and find the ideas challenging and interesting.

References

Brown, B. (2007) *Unlearning Discrimination in the Early Years.* Stoke on Trent: Trentham Books.

Browne, N. (2004) *Gender Equity in the Early Years.* Maidenhead: Open University Press.

Fine, C. (2011) *Delusions of Gender.* London: Icon Books.

Kane, E. (2013) *Rethinking Gender and Sexuality in Childhood.* London: Bloomsbury.

2 | What's it all about?

This chapter introduces you to some of the ideas that will be discussed in this book. You will be asked to think about how children play, your observations of this and what we can learn about children's constructions of gender through these observations. The use of developmentally appropriate practice (DAP) as a way of understanding and planning for children's learning and development is considered and the limitations of this approach as a way of understanding gender are discussed.

You are asked to think about any perceived differences between boys and girls and whether any differences might be due to biology such as hormonal and brain differences or due to the socialisation children receive within their families, early years settings and communities. While acknowledging the importance of both sides of this nature/nurture debate, you will then be asked to consider if there is another way of viewing this issue. Do children have their own power to challenge norms of gender behaviour or are there fixed truths about gender which are beyond challenge?

The chapter ends by considering the difference between sex and gender and some of the complexities that arise from attempts to put people in simplistic categories.

Children at play

It is the morning in an early years setting and the children have recently arrived and chosen what activities they wish to engage with.

The children are all 3 to 4 years old. Lisa is playing with the bricks. She tells her friend Molly that she is building a house for her guinea pig, Squish. Molly sits beside her, picks up a brick and places it next to Lisa's building.

Lisa – No, it can't go there, it's in the way. Squish likes to run so we have to leave lots of room.

Molly – Can I put it here? (Molly holds a brick above one placed by Lisa.)

Lisa – Yes, it can go there. Let's make it higher. That will keep her in.

(Billy joins them and asks what they are doing.)

Molly – We're building a house for Squish.

Billy – Who's Squish?

Lisa – My guinea pig.

Billy – I can build it better. Bigger. I'm stronger.

Lisa – No you can't.

Molly – He can help. Build it up high. Like a tower.

(Billy starts putting bricks on top of Lisa's building. Jack joins them.)

Jack – What you building?

Billy – A tower. Big tall tower. Right up high!

(Billy and Jack add more bricks to the construction. Lisa and Molly wander off. A practitioner notices the building and watches for a while.)

Practitioner – Wow boys! What a tall tower!

How do we understand what happened here as Lisa, Molly, Billy and Jack played with the bricks? What did each child contribute to this activity? What was the adult role? How can we unpick the role that gender played in this exchange between the children and the response from the adult?

Much of our current approach to understanding children's play is to think about it in terms of their development.

Developmentally appropriate practice (DAP)

Many early years practitioners are experienced and committed to providing education for young children based on what they believe to be developmentally appropriate. Observation and assessment lends itself to this approach and the EYFS (DfE 2014) supports it. Blaise (2005) outlines how she used this approach for many years as a kindergarten teacher. She describes how she used observation to enable her to 'know' where each child was developmentally and construct an appropriate curriculum based on that understanding.

DAP draws heavily on the work of Piaget and developmental psychology. Its appeal for many early years practitioners is that it supports child-directed free-play with the role of the adult being to support the naturally occurring developmental pathway of the child.

Believing we know how to construct appropriate practice also enables us to believe we can recognise inappropriate practice. It makes us feel safe and secure in the knowledge that we are using our understanding of the children we work with to provide them with appropriate knowledge and experiences. We can observe the activities that the child takes part in, make judgements about their development and plan accordingly.

If we look at the example above from the perspective of developmentally appropriate practice, we can make several observations about the development of the children involved.

- All four children can concentrate on an activity that interests them.

- All can use language to convey their thoughts.

- They can plan and carry out ideas.

- Lisa makes links between her home environment and the setting.

- Lisa was able to convey her plans to Molly who was able to understand them and join in.

- Billy is confident about his abilities and able to act on his own ideas.

- Molly, Billy and Jack are able to join an activity that is already in progress.

- Billy and Jack are able to take the activity in a new direction that holds interest for them.

- All four children are able to handle and move the bricks confidently and use the space effectively.

- They all use the bricks imaginatively to create constructions that represent their own ideas.

All of these observations fit with the early learning goals of the EYFS (DfE 2014) and are the kind of observations that enable a practitioner to build a picture of a child's development and plan next steps. This might lead to the practitioner planning a range of activities, for example:

- Further opportunities to build and create with a range of construction sets.

- Time for Lisa to share more from home about her guinea pig and other pets.

- Exploring animals and their homes.

- Making the same kind of creations with small bricks to develop fine-motor control.

- Other opportunities for the children to communicate and share ideas.

While all of this is valuable and worthwhile it is also important to think about what this approach might miss. What happened in the observation above that has not been covered when viewing it from the perspective of developmentally appropriate practice? What roles did each child take? What aspect of these roles is influenced by gender? What role did the practitioner take?

By stepping outside developmentally appropriate practice and thinking in a more challenging way, we can see that the play choices of Lisa and Molly were marginalised by Billy and Jack. Billy asserted that he was stronger than the girls and that he could build a bigger, better tower. When Jack joined Billy the activity became focused on building a tower. The house for Squish was lost and Lisa and Molly left the activity. The practitioner praised Billy and Jack for their tall tower.

- What messages do you think these four children would get from this exchange?
- What about any other children who saw or heard what happened?
- What ethos would this create for other practitioners in the setting?
- What would it say to parents if one of the children told them what happened?

If this was an isolated incident it would have limited impact on the children but if events like this are a regular occurrence in the setting, the children will absorb the unspoken messages conveyed in this incident. Even though they may not be able to put it into words, they would slowly develop an understanding that the boys have more power especially with activities such as the large construction sets. The girls might feel that their ideas and plans are of less importance than the boys and that the boys get more praise.

Are girls and boys different?

When asked this question, a group of early years practitioners had the following discussion:

Practitioner 1 – Well, they are born different aren't they?

P2 – I notice in my setting that the girls do tend to be quieter and the boys are a bit more . . . well . . . boisterous!

P3 – Yeah but they might have learned some of that as they are treated differently.

P1 – Are they? Or is it that people respond to them differently because they are different? I mean, they have a different biology and their hormones are different.

P3 – I think those differences are exaggerated. Also, all the pink stuff is quite new. My mum says that when she was a child there wasn't nearly as much difference as there is now.

P2 – That's true, maybe some of it is learned. We accept that children are like sponges in other areas of learning so why not this? But I still think there are some biological differences.

P4 – I think it's impossible to know. I think it is a shame that children's opportunities are sometimes limited by what is expected of boys and girls. If all children had exactly the same opportunities it might be easier to see if any differences are innate.

P5 – I'm sorry but I just think they are different. I've got my own children as well as working with children. I've got a son and a daughter and they've just been different from day one. My daughter shows no interest in playing with her brother's toys and the same the other way round.

P3 – In some ways I think this question is impossible to answer and the important thing for us as early years practitioners is to give all children opportunities to explore as wide a range of activities and experiences as possible.

P5 – I agree but I don't think you can change nature.

What do you think about this discussion? Did you identify with any of the comments more than others? A good place to start when thinking about gender in early childhood is to try to unpick your own beliefs. You are then in a good position to start discussing them and, possibly, to challenge them. You will also then be more informed when you read about different explanations for perceived differences between genders.

Biology

Science is seen as objective and provable and, therefore, is a powerful discourse in many aspects of our drive to understand society. It is easy to feel that if something is shown to be true by clear scientific evidence then it is beyond challenge. There are many studies that provide 'proof' that girls and boys are biologically different. This is nowhere more true than in studies of brain differences between boys and girls in early childhood (Browne 2004). While it may no longer be the case that science is used to suggest that brain differences prove that men are more intelligent than women, the idea of there being differences still carries power. One of the most widely held views of differences between male and female brains that is currently popular with the general public and appears to have a scientific basis is the idea of left brain/right brain dominance. The left hemisphere is seen as the centre for language and speech while the right hemisphere is where we process space and shape (Browne 2004). Some studies appear to show gender differences in the dominance of the left or right brain (Kimura 1969; Coltheart et al. 1975; Corsi-Cabrera et al. 1989; Meyers-Levy 1994 all cited in Browne 2004) although much of this has been disputed as the sample studies were often small, carried out on the brains of elderly deceased people or damaged brains after death.

Despite these criticisms the view of left brain/right brain dominance and of gender based brain differences generally remains strong and is often used as a way of supporting our understanding of differences between girls and boys in terms of educational provision and achievement.

In criticising the over formalisation of early education Katz (2015) states that formal instruction 'is more damaging to boys than girls'. She suggests that one possible explanation for this is 'the well-known fact that girls mature neurologically slightly earlier than boys' (Katz 2015: 3). Even though she is offering a *possible* explanation, she asserts it as a 'well-known fact'. We may, at the very least, need to keep our minds open about what may or may not be fact in relation to gender differences between young children.

What differences between girls and boys do you think might be caused by biology? When asked this question, a group of early years practitioners answered with the following areas and thoughts:

* Language development. Girls are more advanced with language skills than boys of the same age.

- Ability to sit still. Boys are more active than girls. Girls can concentrate for longer.

- Girls can deal with emotions more maturely. Boys tend to get more angry or rough.

- Boys find it harder to develop empathy for others and are more competitive.

- Boys and girls play differently. Girls are more likely to play quietly while boys like to run around and play at superheroes.

- Boys are more aggressive and girls are more passive.

What are your responses to these statements? Have you observed these differences in your setting? Do you tend to think they have a biological cause? Even if we feel certain that these differences between girls and boys are real, can we be sure they are caused by biological differences?

The difficulty with the biological argument is that through this lens, gender behaviour is seen as fixed and unchangeable. If it were the case that being female or male was a biological given we wouldn't see the variation that we do between individuals and between cultures. Blaise (2005) also argues that if biology were the only driving force, we would not see the changes that have taken place over time. As Blaise suggests, being female in the present day is not the same as it was 50 years ago.

Socialisation

If notions of appropriate gender behaviour change over time and vary between cultures, it is reasonable to argue that there is something else going on here. From this perspective children are socialised in to what is seen as appropriate gender roles by imitation and reinforcement. Known as social learning or socialisation theory the suggestion is that children pick up cues from the people around them as they develop their understanding of how to become a girl or a boy. It is seen as the process by which children learn to conform to social norms (James et al. 1998).

If we return to the example above, we see the subtle messages the children receive. The boys receive praise for their tall tower while the girls give up their attempts to build a home for the guinea pig and quietly leave the activity. There are many ways in which society indicates to children what it means to have a particular gender:

> We dress and ornament boys and girls differently, teach them to behave differently, offer them different opportunities and obstacles, treat them differently in a host of ways and emphasize gender to them as a socially important category. Then we interpret the resulting patterns of gendered identity, attributes and behaviours as confirmation that they were different to begin with.
>
> (Kane 2013: 13)

MacNaughton refers to this theory as 'the sponge model of identity formation' (2000: 18). There is simplicity to this view as it is easy to see how it could make sense of what we observe in young children. If children see their parents behaving in gendered ways, it is clear that this will have an impact on their children. If the father goes out to work and the mother is the one doing the caring and nurturing, it is likely that the children will see this as their model of how to behave, especially as this is supported by the many images around young children on the television, in advertising, in toy packaging and in many other forms of marketing. The positive aspect of this view is that it provides hope that if children are exposed to a range of behaviours, they will learn from that and grow up with a greater sense of choice. A weakness of this view though is that the adults (the ones 'doing' the socialisation) are seen as active and powerful while the children (the ones 'receiving' the socialisation) are seen as passive and powerless.

MacNaughton suggests that socialisation theory sees the child as having 'little or no ability to do other than think and feel what he or she is told by society' (2000: 20).

Moving on from biological and socialisation theories

There is no doubt that biology and socialisation play a role in the development of gender roles. However, what is ignored in these explanations is the child's own agency and power and the dynamic between this and the power held by others in settings, families, communities and society as a whole. As Blaise argues, these views fail to recognise that 'children are active, that they can make decisions and choices, and that they have the ability to resist and challenge adults' (2005: 13).

Let's return to Lisa, Molly, Billy and Jack.

Lisa and Molly have wandered off from the construction area and are in the mark making area. Lisa tells Molly she is drawing a picture of the house she wanted to build for Squish.

Lisa – It has lots of rooms and it has a bed here with straw so he is cosy.

Molly – If we built it, what could we use for straw?

Lisa – There is straw for the rabbits.

Lisa and Molly go and ask a practitioner if they can have some straw. They explain what happened with the house they were building. Billy and Jack are still in the construction area although they are now building a road by laying bricks end to end. The practitioner encourages Lisa and Molly to share their plans with Billy and Jack.

Lisa – We were building a house and you made it into a tower. We didn't want a tower.

Billy – Now we're making a road.

Molly – We don't want a road.

Jack – How would you get to the house then?

Molly – Yeah, we could have a house and a road.

Lisa – The road could lead to the house!

Practitioner – Can you work together to build the house and the road?

Billy – Yeah!

Lisa – Okay. You build the road over there coming up here and the house can be here.

The children work together on the construction. Billy and Jack continue building their road although they change the direction of the bricks so that it leads to where Lisa pointed. Lisa and Molly start to lay out the outline of the house. The practitioner gives them some straw and they explain to Billy and Jack that it is so they can make Squish a bed.

- In what ways can we view this second sequence as the four children continued their play with the bricks?
- Do you still see gendered play here?
- What roles did each of the children take?
- Were there any challenges to gender roles?
- What role did the practitioner take?

You may feel that the children were still playing in a gendered way. The boys were building a road and the girls were building a house and were concerned about creating a cosy bed for Squish. However, if we look more deeply at the whole play episode between the four children we can see that there were some shifts and changes. Initially the boys took over the construction area and the plans the girls had were marginalised. The practitioner missed that this is what had happened and praised the boys for their construction. The girls moved to the mark making area but didn't let go of their desire to build Squish a house. By explaining what had happened to the practitioner, they managed to re-engage with the boys and turn the play back to their original plan. Billy and Jack continued to build their road but changed its direction to fit in with the girls' plan to build the house.

These shifts and changes can seem minor and are easy to miss but they are vitally important signs of children expressing their own sense of power and they often include significant challenges to perceived norms of gendered behaviour.

At this point you may find it helpful to revisit some of your own observations or carry out some new ones and think about gender as you watch the children play and negotiate roles.

- What do you see that conforms to stereotypically gendered play?

- What do you see that challenges this?

- Which is more obvious and which is more hidden?

It may well be that you find it easier to notice the play that conforms to gender stereotypes. Just as with the children, you will have been soaking up messages about how boys and girls should behave since you were a child yourself and this could influence what you look for in the play of the children in your setting. When children are very non-conforming this can be clearly obvious too. It is likely that a boy who likes dressing up as a princess or a girl who likes climbing and riding bikes will be noticed and commented on. What can be more challenging is to notice the subtle shifts such as with the example above. In order to do this you need to look closely at your own practice, think reflectively about your own views and ideas and be open to looking at the way children play with fresh eyes.

The difficulty with the biological and socialisation views of gender is that it discourages this examination. Neither view offers an explanation of why children challenge perceived gender norms and neither view recognises the power and agency of the child.

In search of 'truth'

People tend to like truth. We like to believe that we can 'know' things for certain and there are fixed aspects to human life that we can observe and then respond to. If we return to the conversation between the practitioners above we can clearly see this, particularly with Practitioner 5 who says 'I'm sorry but I just think [boys and girls] are different' and 'I don't think you can change nature'. If the way boys and girls think and behave is fixed and there is an essential truth to this then all practitioners need to do is think about how to respond to this.

Similarly, if we are certain that children are socialised into gender roles by their families and other cultural influences then we are also certain that children only have a passive role to play in this. As discussed above, socialisation theory is very persuasive and easily becomes seen as a 'truth'. Wolpert invites us to 'use these truths to counteract the stereotypes' (2005: 30). She then goes on to assert that:

> Gender identity is learned through culture rather than being primarily a function of physical gender. If biology were the primary determinant, then we would not be able to find gender role differences existing by ethnic or national culture, as indeed they do. Females and males act differently in different cultures, depending on what has been defined as gender appropriate in that culture.
>
> (Wolpert 2005: 30)

Declaring something as a 'truth' gives it authority and power. To see this truth as natural and neutral is to simply accept things as they are (MacNaughton 2005) and leaves the power relations within that unchallenged. While it may be true that there are cultural differences in relation to gender roles, there are still many differences between people *within* a culture and this is not explained by socialisation theory.

To start to think differently about children, childhood and issues such as gender can initially be uncomfortable. It is far easier to imagine that there is truth than to question this and be open to the challenges this presents.

The challenge to the idea of a fixed truth is an aspect of 'poststructuralism' which is an approach that acknowledges the uncertainties of life and does not assume there are fixed realities waiting to be uncovered. The work of Foucault is crucial here and although Foucault did not himself apply his theories to early childhood, others have (Blaise 2005; Browne 2004; MacNaughton 2005; MacNaughton 2000; Martin 2011).

The Foucauldian perspective argues against the developmentalism looked at above. The Piagetian view that children develop along fixed trajectories allows dominant discourses about gender and other areas of inequality to remain unaddressed (Martin 2011). MacNaughton (2005) suggests that trying to understand children's lives from multiple perspectives allows us to question this notion of 'truth' and to challenge the power imbalances between groups.

From the moment a baby is born we are aware of gender. Often the first question asked is 'Is it a boy or a girl?' For many people the answer to this question is the crucial beginning to decisions about names, clothes, toys and ways of being with the baby. Expectations are based on the views we hold about girls and boys in terms of temperament, behaviour, interests and play preferences. Even very young children have deep and complex understandings about gender and they bring these understandings with them into early years settings. Developmentalism can confirm the way early years settings operate in relation to gender. If power relations aren't questioned children may unconsciously assume they are acceptable.

Consider the following play situations:

- A group of three-year-old girls are playing in the role-play area. A two-year-old boy observes them but soon wanders off.

- In the outdoor area there are three large wheeled toys. All are occupied by boys.

- Boys and girls are playing together in the sand tray. Four dinosaurs are in the tray along with pebbles, sticks and shells. Two boys are playing with the dinosaurs while two girls line up the pebbles and shells and make patterns in the sand with the sticks.

- In the writing area a group of girls are drawing. They are talking to each other as they draw.

What do you notice about the gendered play taking place in these scenarios? Why might the younger boy have wandered away from the role-play area? How would a girl feel if she wanted a turn on the wheeled toys and how would a boy feel if he wanted to join the drawing activity? What gendered activity is still taking place even when children are playing together in the sand tray?

Martin (2011) analysed the use of space in a nursery and found that boys dominated indoor and outdoor construction areas, climbing frames and specific sports equipment such as baseball nets while girls dominated writing areas, collage tables and indoor and outdoor role-play areas. She found that the children played predominantly in single-sex groups and that they learned what knowledge was important in order to belong to these groups. Her research shows that while practitioners may support a child who acts outside these roles, they rarely actively challenge the roles themselves. She suggests that many practitioners see their role as supporting developmentally appropriate practice and that from this perspective children are simply choosing to engage with the activities they prefer.

By seeing gender as a fixed truth and the way children behave as being part of that truth, we absolve ourselves from any responsibility to think and act differently in our relationships with children.

Boys and girls, male and female, sex and gender

We often think in an either/or way about many issues and categorise things into opposites. Even when we don't necessarily see things as opposite, we use the terms in that way. We talk of a person seeing something in black and white; of our moods being up and down; there is night and day; good and bad; rich and poor and, of course, man and woman and gay and straight. We talk of all these things as if there is nothing in between.

(Price and Tayler 2015: 20)

This binary way of thinking means that we have very fixed categories and that we see ourselves, other adults and the children we work with as either male or female. Often gender ambiguity is found to be disturbing and challenging. It is experienced as uncomfortable if we cannot tell if someone is male or female.

Imagine for a moment welcoming new children into a setting without knowing whether they are girls or boys. While this is an entirely hypothetical scenario it is worth considering your reactions to this. Put aside the fact that what children are called and how they dress generally tells us whether they are girls or boys, consider what it would be like and what differences it might make to your practice not to know a child's gender.

- Would it change how you spoke to them?
- Would it alter the activities you would expect them to engage with?
- What differences would it make to your registration forms?
- Would it make a difference to how you engaged with the parents?
- Do you think it might change the way the children related to each other?
- What might your expectations be in terms of free-flow provision?
- What differences would it make generally to your practice?

Many practitioners might feel that it would make no difference and that they are gender neutral in how they relate to the children in their care. Some very honest reflection needs to take place in order to be able to think about your own practice in this area.

An important distinction here is to separate our understanding of sex and gender. Sex is biologically determined and generally relates to the external sexual characteristics seen at birth. From this a baby is declared either a boy or a girl. Gender is the social construction that is built on this and, while the jury is still out on the relationship between the two, there is no doubt that a child is surrounded by messages about what it means to be a boy or a girl from birth.

Occasionally a baby is born with the external sexual characteristics of both male and female. This is known as intersex and usually decisions are quickly made about whether the child should be male or female and surgery is used to create this. There is considerable controversy about this and cases where the child grows up with a very strong sense of being in the wrong body. Sometimes the situation comes to light at puberty when the young person develops the secondary sexual characteristics of the opposite sex.

As society is largely built around the binary ideal, the difficulties for intersex people start at birth with whether to put male or female on the birth certificate. Some countries such as Germany have changed the law so that this is no longer a requirement, enabling families to take time to consider their options.

> Being Intersex is not a disease, it is not a 'disorder', it is a perfectly normal – and actually quite common – variation within human development. In reality, the term 'Intersex' is an invention, only made necessary by society's insistence on maintaining the rigid classification of all human beings into the two inflexible stereotypes of 'male' or 'female'.
>
> (UKIA 2015)

The construction of a male or female gender does not always fit with a person's internal sense of who they are. A transgender person is someone 'whose gender identity does not conform to the gender category they were assigned at birth' (Kane 2013: 53). For a child growing up as either male or female but feeling that that is not who they are this can be a complex and distressing time for the child and the family. As the child becomes older many issues will need to be addressed with schools such as what the child wears, what toilet the child uses and how the child will be addressed. (Case study 4.1 in Chapter 4 looks at the way a school supported a transgender child.)

In the context of this book, we are talking about very young children and we suggest that the approach should be to provide *all* children with choices about how they dress, how they play, how they behave and how they engage with others. Any questions children may have about gender are best answered honestly and openly and children who appear to be exploring gender in a way that may not conform to the gender assigned at birth should be supported in this as they would with any other area of their development.

Conclusion

This chapter has asked you to think about some complex issues and you have been encouraged to think about everyday practice with the children you work with in ways which might appear new and challenging. You might be used to thinking about how children learn and develop in terms of providing developmentally appropriate practice that helps you to consider where the child is and what their next steps might be.

The case study referred to throughout this chapter will hopefully have enabled you to consider other ways of thinking about your practice in relation to gender. You have been asked to consider the idea that there is not necessarily a fixed truth about how gender is constructed and that young children have their own agency and power that enables them to challenge expected behaviour. You have been encouraged to think about how your responses and interactions with children will have an impact on how children build on their sense of power.

The discussions have been supported with an explanation of what some of the terms used throughout the book mean and you may find it helpful to return to this as you read the rest of the book.

References

Blaise, M. (2005) *Playing it Straight: Uncovering Gender Discourses in the Early Childhood Classroom*. Abingdon: Routledge.

Browne, N. (2004) *Gender Equity in the Early Years*. Maidenhead: Open University Press.

Department for Education (DfE) (2014) *Statutory Framework for the Early Years Foundation Stage*. London: DfE.

James, A. Jenks, C. and Prout, A. (1998) *Theorizing Childhood*. Cambridge: Polity Press.

Kane, E. (2013) *Rethinking Gender and Sexuality in Childhood*. London: Bloomsbury.

Katz, L. (2015) *Lively Minds: Distinctions Between Academic Versus Intellectual Goals for Young Children*. University of Illinois: Defending the Early Years.

MacNaughton, G. (2000) *Rethinking Gender in Early Childhood Education*. London: Sage.

MacNaughton, G. (2005) *Doing Foucault in Early Childhood Studies*. Oxon: Routledge.

Martin, B. (2011) *Children at Play: Learning Gender in the Early Years*. London: Trentham.

Price, D. and Tayler, K. (2015) *LGBT Diversity and Inclusion in Early Years Education*. London: Routledge.

UKIA (2015) *The UK Intersex Association* [Online]. Available at www.ukia. co.uk/about.html (accessed 1 July 2015).

Wolpert, E. (2005) *Start Seeing Diversity*. Boston: Redleaf Press.

3 Legislative background

We discuss in our previous book *LGBT Diversity and Inclusion in Early Years Education* (Price and Tayler 2015) that legislation and guidance can be viewed by early years practitioners as interference from outside agencies. It can also be seen as a way of imposing unnecessary bureaucracy on the relationship that exists between the practitioner and the child (Price and Tayler 2015). In looking at a contradiction to these views we consider in this chapter how current legislation is merely a reflection of the way that society views an issue at a particular time in history. Legislation starts with a societal change in thinking about a particular issue and makes that change in attitude progress to a change in law. A good illustration of this is the Sexual Offences Act 1967 which decriminalised homosexual acts in private between two men over the age of 21 and was a mirror of the way in which many people in the UK at that time regarded gay men. The legislation caught up with the way that public thinking had changed over time. Of course sometimes laws are made in opposition to large sections of public opinion, for example the Welfare Bill 2015 that disproportionally impacts on women and children.

Because legislation has to be put into practice after it has been made law, there has to be a way of making sure it is adhered to. For example, as a result of the Children Act 1989 there were many registration and inspection units set up around the UK to ensure that daycare facilities were registered and inspected in the way that the Act had outlined.

In this chapter we aim to give some historical background to the legislation that surrounds gender and also to discuss the current legislation that practitioners need to be aware of in their workplace.

Historical background

We start this section with a further illustration of this link between changing public opinion and legislation in connection with considering gender. There are many examples of this we could give when thinking of the ways in which changing attitudes towards women have been represented in legislation. We could, for example, think about the right to vote or abortion as instances where legislation has evolved and changed through time and in response to societal change.

Our first example looks at the right of women to own property.

Activity

To start this reflection we would ask you to consider the following legislation and its repeal:

> 1870 The Married Women's Property Act allows married women to own their own property. Previously, when women married, their property transferred to their husbands. Divorce heavily favoured men, allowing property to remain in their possession. This act allows women to keep their property, married, divorced, single or widowed.
> (Manchester Metropolitan University 2015)

This is an indication that, at that time, there was a move towards extending the rights of women and this move was part of a general shift towards gender equality that is continuing today and encompasses such issues as equal pay, voting rights, access to abortion and protection from domestic abuse. These legislations have come about as a result of the actions of brave women (and men) with a strong sense of social injustice and an urge to change an area of discrimination.

The legislation also can show a shift in the thinking of society in other areas that have permeated to gender issues. Many of the forward thinking social reformist Acts in the 1960s that related to sexuality are linked to the more general change in society, the 'permissive' 60s as we now think of it. This in turn is linked to a post World War Two openness to new ideas and ways of being.

We also need to remind you that what we are discussing are rights that women hold in the UK and are not always accepted in the same way worldwide. There are still areas of the world where women do not have the basic rights that women expect in the UK. An example of this is the United Nations Treaty of 1981 that sought to eliminate all forms of discrimination against women; note the updated map of the countries that did not sign or who are still seeking changes before they sign (United Nations 1981).

In the UK there is still a disparity in the wages that women and men receive for the same job, and this pay gap between men and women is actually getting larger in recent years. This refutes the commonly held myth that women have successfully achieved complete parity professionally with men. As a point of interest there has been a recent initiative by the previous coalition government, initially resisted by the Conservative Party, for larger companies to publish details of any difference in the wages that they pay men and women (Morris 2015). The resistance to the move to 'name and shame' the companies – at first from the government and also from employers – shows us that, at the time of writing this book, there are still live and current gender issues that are ongoing battles to be won and legislation that needs to be written, passed through Parliament and put into place.

Morris (2015) also points out that the recent anti-austerity measures have a greater impact on women as they make up a larger section of the public services workforce and this is an area that has been affected by cuts. Lower wages and part-time wages lead to lower pensions and savings and this has an impact as women grow older and leave the workforce.

At the time of writing a new comparison of wages of men and women in management shows that because of the pay gap women work an average of one hundred minutes a day 'for free' (Spencer 2015).

Reflecting on this, and thinking about the future leaders, employers and shapers of society who we care for in early years settings must inform the important gender work that we carry out with young children. It must show us the importance of this crucial underpinning of attitudes and influences that children receive in the early years.

In *Leading and Supporting Early Years Teams* there is a chapter on the legislative background to current professional practice and policy and a discussion about the way that the early years workforce is mainly staffed by women and the range of reasons that there could be for this (Price and Ota 2014).

In the workforce women often take leave of absence for motherhood and other caring roles and this impacts on their ability to be promoted, attend training, gain experience and qualifications and improve their job prospects generally. While working and trying to manage these caring roles women can face discrimination and negative attitudes from colleagues and employers. These attitudes can happen even when women are not actually caring but there is a perception that they will. Rather like when we were at school and it was thought a waste of time for us to have jobs as we would just leave them to get married and have babies.

This is referred to as the 'Motherhood Penalty' and is an umbrella term to refer to the fact that women are generally the main carers for children. Because of the attitude to this important job by some employers as a result women can miss out on training opportunities, pay rises, career progression and promotions. This injustice and disparity is based on the poor value that is given to the crucial work of raising the next generation. We would argue that this is because it is seen as a 'natural' work that women are genetically more pre-disposed to do and so the status of it is not as high as the 'professional' work that is seen to need training and education in order to 'master' – and the ultimate statement about that is in the last word that we have used.

As a final remark on legislation that affects women we would ask you to think about the number of women that there are in Parliament. There was a rise in the last election – May 2015 – and this was the biggest rise since 1997. There are 191 women MPs out of a possible

650. If it is accepted that women constitute roughly 50 per cent of the population then it is clear that, even with the positive recent rise of a third in numbers, there is not a representative amount of women in Parliament that reflects the number of women in the UK. So any legislation that affects women is written and enacted by a Parliament that is mostly comprised of men. For the first time in history the opposition now have more women than men in their cabinet.

Twofold responsibility

As in most legislation that surrounds early years work there is a twofold responsibility that rests on the shoulders of the managers and owners of settings – the children and the employees. This is reiterated in the Ofsted handbook that guides inspectors.

> In addition to meeting the EYFS requirements providers must also comply with other relevant legislation. This includes safeguarding legislation and legislation relating to employment, anti-discrimination, health and safety and data collection. Where the inspector identifies concerns that may also relate to other legislation s/he must notify the appropriate team in Ofsted, who will decide what action should be taken and whether there should be liaison with the appropriate agencies.
>
> (Ofsted 2015: 15)

The children who attend the setting

The first responsibility that the setting has is towards the children they care for who attend the setting. The care and education of the children who attend the setting is guided by the legislative directives that underpin the responsibilities towards them in matters of education and welfare. These directives stem from the Early Years Foundation Stage. The EYFS is referred to in the most recent childcare legislation – the Children and Families Act 2014.

Equality of opportunity and anti-discriminatory practice, ensuring that every child is included and supported.

(Department for Education 2014: 5)

This is one of the underpinning four statements that the EYFS is based on. The EYFS and its non-statutory accompaniment *Development Matters* do not specifically mention gender or providing an environment that is supportive to young children exploring gender roles (Early Education 2012). However, many of the statements that are made have this sensitive understanding as an unspoken prerequisite for many of the requirements. For example from the section in *Development Matters* on 'making relationships' this is the statement regarding how adults could encourage children between 30–50 months in this:

Support children in developing positive relationships by challenging negative comments and actions towards either peers or adults.

(Early Education 2012: 9)

We think that encouraging children to talk freely about gender roles in a positive way and providing positive role models and an enabling environment would be part of this adult led task.

Ofsted

The responsibility of providers to ensure that they are supporting children with positive discussions and role models about gender and providing an enabling environment that helps this process is not specifically commented on in the Ofsted framework as we have already noted in the EYFS. However, as with the EYFS, there are some overarching statements that we feel can be underpinned by the work that we are suggesting here. For example, in the *Inspection Handbook*, an outstanding provision has this said about it:

The extremely sharp focus on helping them to acquire communication and language skills, and on supporting their physical, personal, social and emotional development helps all children make rapid improvement in their learning from their starting points.

(Ofsted 2015: 34)

We feel that if children are being supported in having open discussions about gender and the choices that they are making then it feeds into their healthy emotional development. A practical example of this would be the little boy who is able to play with dolls and dressing-up clothes without being steered away from them as not being gender suitable for him. We refer to incidents like this many times in other chapters.

We also draw your attention to the wellbeing section that states

The effectiveness of care practices in helping children feel emotionally secure and ensuring that children are physically and emotionally healthy.

(Ofsted 2015: 36)

Again, we believe that an enabling environment that supports the choices that children make without stereotyping is part of the work that is needed in order to help children feel good about themselves.

An outstanding provision in terms of wellbeing meets the following criteria:

Care practices are better than good because:

- All practitioners are highly skilled and sensitive in helping children of all ages form secure emotional attachments, and provide a strong base for helping them in developing their independence and ability to explore.
- Children increasingly show high levels of self-control during activities and confidence in social situations, and are developing an excellent understanding of how to manage risks and challenges relative to their age.
- Children's safety and safeguarding is central to everything all practitioners do. They effectively support children's growing understanding of how to keep themselves safe and healthy.

- There is a highly stimulating environment with child-accessible resources that promote learning and challenge children both in and outdoors.
- The strong skills of all key persons ensure all children are emotionally well prepared for the next stages in their learning. Practitioners skilfully support children's transitions both within the setting and to other settings and school.

(Ofsted 2015: 37)

Activity

Can you see how the enabling environment that we have described in this book supports children in achieving the outcomes above? You might want to think of one thing that your team does at the moment that is outstanding in terms of this practice in relation to gender and one thing that you could move forward.

Discussion

We would ask you to think especially about bullet points one, two and four. We discuss elsewhere in this book the physical constraints that society can place on girls in terms of risk and physical activity. We would ask you to critically examine your own practice in terms of thinking that girls shouldn't be as physically adventurous as boys.

The employees in the setting

The second responsibility of the manager of the setting is to comply with employment and other legislation that protects and supports the adults who work in the setting. The Equality Act 2010 brought together a range of other Acts that were part of the range of equalities law that protected the rights of the more vulnerable members of society. These were previously 'stand alone' Acts such as the Disability

Discrimination Act 2005, and after the Equality Act there were some enhancements made to the different Acts and they were conveniently put together.

The Equality Act is a mixture of rights and responsibilities that have:

- **Stayed the same** – for example, direct discrimination still occurs when 'someone is treated less favorably than another person because of a protected characteristic'
- **Changed** – for example, employees will now be able to complain of harassment even if it is not directed at them, if they can demonstrate that it creates an offensive environment for them
- **Been extended** – for example, associative discrimination (direct discrimination against someone because they associate with another person who possesses a protected characteristic) will cover age, disability, gender reassignment and sex as well as race, religion and belief and sexual orientation
- **Been introduced for the first time** – for example, the concept of discrimination arising from disability, which occurs if a disabled person is treated unfavourably because of something arising in consequence of their disability.

(ACAS 2011)

There are nine protected characteristics that are listed in the Equality Act and where discrimination can be legally challenged in terms of the rights and responsibilities above. The protected characteristics are:

- Age
- Disability
- Gender reassignment
- Marriage and civil partnership
- Pregnancy and maternity
- Race
- Religion and belief
- Sex
- Sexual orientation.

(Equality and Human Rights Commission 2015)

People who have or are associated with someone who falls under one of the above characteristics are protected from discrimination and harassment by law. In terms of gender we would say that pregnancy and maternity and gender reassignment stand out as the protected characteristics that we would be discussing here, although there are crossovers as well.

Activity

An interesting activity for a staff meeting would be to look at the two protected characteristics that we have highlighted and discuss possible case studies that might arise when a staff member could have a case for discrimination in law, for example someone being passed over for promotion or training because they were pregnant and just about to go on maternity leave.

Another possibility would be someone not being offered a job because they had had gender reassignment.

Discussion

Talk within the team about reactions to this. Do team members think that it is fair that there are protected characteristics? Would they see that the examples above are justly legal cases where employers could be taken to task for their actions? In order to fully comply with legislation it is important that staff members understand and support the duty that they have under the Act to behave in a way that doesn't discriminate against anyone who has, or is associated with, one of the protected characteristics.

Team members are also responsible for their actions in relation to discrimination and the responsibility doesn't just rest on the shoulders of the management team. Having these frank, and sometimes difficult, conversations is important in order to create a shared responsibility and adherence to legal obligations.

Nation states

Northern Ireland

All of these different nation states have their own childcare guidance that differs from England's EYFS in some aspects. Until the last revision of the EYFS England had a direct mention of good equalities practice in the standards but this has not been included in the 2014 version of the guidance. We still feel that it is a crucial element in supporting children's rights and wishes and underpins the educational targets that the current EYFS stresses. That is why we have unpicked the EYFS and looked at places where good equalities practice, including gender, is in our opinion in the background of many of the statements made – almost like the 'hidden curriculum'.

Northern Ireland has a clear statement about gender included in their curriculum for early years:

> Children should have opportunities to explore situations, express feelings in a way that is not gender specific and challenge stereo-types. Do not confine children to any one type of role-play, and encourage both sexes to take on leadership roles and talk with adults about traditional and non-traditional roles. Boys and girls should be encouraged to play with the full range of toys and equipment available to them in the setting. Routines should be organised in a way that is not gender specific.
>
> (Northern Ireland Department of Education 2012: 15)

This is an example of the type of clear ethos that we would like to see included in the English EYFS and shows that Northern Ireland wish to spearhead good practice in gender by showing that this type of supportive role by early years staff is an integral part of the expectations of day-to-day activities and conversations that should be happening in a daycare setting.

Scotland

Education in Scotland has a whole curriculum for children and young people aged three to eighteen. There is more detailed separate guidance for birth to three and then from three to eighteen. The guidance in Scotland, in contrast to England's EYFS, has more mention of inclusion, and therefore gender, when discussing children's individual needs and rights and the importance of supporting them. The guidance has a strong emphasis on

> Dignity, privacy, choice, safety, realising potential, and equality and diversity
>
> (Education Scotland 2015a: 19)

We believe that making these expectations of inclusion in terms of equality and diversity explicit in the guidance from the very outset provides a good foundation for best practice when supporting children with exploring gender.

> Awareness of the significance of children's life circumstances, for example their socio-economic status, race, gender, disability, religion, or whether they are looked after, is vital in helping staff to get it right for every child. All adults working with Scotland's youngest children must demonstrate, through their practice, their awareness that every child has the right to a positive start in life through respectful relationships, which show responsive care. In this way Scotland's youngest children can be nurtured to develop a capacity for love, empathy, respect, resilience, positive relationships and the chance to succeed.
>
> (Education Scotland 2015b: 13–16)

It is clear to us that an enabling environment with respectful adults who affirm children's choices and discussions is an important part of this nurturing process. The Scottish standards have a very positive emphasis on respect and the importance of the adults who care for children understanding what this means in terms of valuing diversity and listening to children's views and wishes in a range of ways that are age appropriate.

The guidance for three to eighteen years is based on a structure of four capabilities as outlined in Table 3.1.

Looking at this it reminds us of the 'Every Child Matters' structure that used to inform the standards in the UK and we can see that the section that is labelled 'confidant individuals' and 'responsible adults' contains much in it that could link to gender.

Wales

The Welsh early years curriculum has strong opening statements that emphasise the fundamental importance of inclusion and diversity to the education and care of young children. There is also an area of learning that is entitled 'Personal and social development, well-being and cultural diversity'.

Personal and Social Development, Well-being and Cultural Diversity is at the heart of the Foundation Phase and children's skills are developed across all Areas of Learning through participation in experiential learning activities indoors and outdoors. Children learn about themselves, their relationships with other children and adults both within and beyond the family. They are encouraged to develop their self-esteem, their personal beliefs and moral values. They develop an understanding that others have differing needs, abilities, beliefs and views. The Foundation Phase supports the cultural identity of all children, to celebrate different cultures and help children recognise and gain a positive awareness of their own and other cultures. Positive attitudes should be developed to enable children to become increasingly aware of, and appreciate the value of, the diversity of cultures and languages that exist in a multicultural Wales. They should become increasingly aware of the traditions and celebrations that are important aspects of the cultures within Wales.

Table 3.1   The four capabilities

Successful learners	Confident individuals	Responsible citizens	Effective contributors
Attributes	Attributes	Attributes	Attributes
• enthusiasm and motivation for learning	• self-respect	• respect for others	• an enterprising attitude
• determination to reach high standards of achievement	• a sense of physical, mental and emotional well-being	• commitment to participate responsibly in political, economic, social and cultural life	• resilience
• openness to new thinking and ideas	• secure values and beliefs	Capabilities	• self-reliance
Capabilities	• ambition	• develop knowledge and understanding of the world and Scotland's place in it	Capabilities
• use literacy, communication and numeracy skills	Capabilities	• understand different beliefs and cultures	• communicate in different ways and in different settings
• use technology for learning	• relate to others and manage themselves	• make informed choices and decisions	• work in partnership and in teams
• think creatively and independently	• pursue a healthy and active lifestyle	• evaluate environmental, scientific and technological issues	• take the initiative and lead
• learn independently and as part of a group	• be self-aware	• develop informed, ethical views of complex issues	• apply critical thinking in new contexts
• make reasoned evaluations	• develop and communicate their own beliefs and view of the world		• create and develop
• link and apply different kinds of learning in new situations	• live as independently as they can		• solve problems
	• assess risk and make informed decisions		
	• achieve success in different areas of activity		

(Education Scotland 2015b)

Motivation and commitment to learning is encouraged, as children begin to understand their own potential and capabilities. Children are supported in becoming confident, competent and independent thinkers and learners. They develop an awareness of their environment and learn about the diversity of people who live and work there. Positive attitudes for enjoying and caring for their environment are fostered. As their self-identity develops, children begin to express their feelings and to empathise with others. They experience challenges that extend their learning.

(Welsh Government 2015)

We have reproduced this statement in its entirety as we feel it is an important establishment of key principles of respectful engagement with young children and must include discussion and exploration of gender roles with children as part of its brief. The curriculum is currently being updated but the area of learning that focuses on well-being and diversity is still being included so there is every indication that there will still be a strong emphasis on diversity and respecting children's individual personalities and wishes.

Activity

We have included links to all of the different frameworks we have looked at in this section in the list of references and we would encourage you to look at all frameworks and see if there are aspects of them that you would want included in a future revision of the one that you work with. There also might be some useful directions contained in them that you could look at in order to inform and extend your own practice in aspects of gender. Printing out sections of these alternative curriculums with the EYFS and giving them to a staff team to cut and paste their own curriculum would be an interesting activity for a staff training session.

Some of the curriculum that we have included breaks the area of learning into range and skills. This is much in the same way that 'Development Matters' does. We would encourage you to research this further and see where the differences and similarities are with the EYFS and think reflectively about the way that it would be useful to break a new curriculum into different areas. Finally we would ask you to think about the learning theories that might underpin a statutory curriculum – can you see anything in the guidance that has been influenced by the thinking of Piaget or Vygotsky for example?

Conclusion

From this chapter we hope that you have received a snapshot of the historical and current legislation surrounding women's rights in employment and property and an understanding of the current legislation that is embedded in early years work and its workforce.

Importantly we have aimed to present an understanding of where legislation comes from and the way that it is meshed into the attitudes of society and not merely imposed by an outside body.

Legislation that has been passed through Parliament is the end result of a long process of governments making a judgement on current public opinion and then consulting those people who they believe represent that opinion. Documents then have to be drafted, altered and negotiated in order to ensure that the Act reaches majority agreement before it can be passed as law.

When legislation becomes law it has to be enforced and monitored by a range of public bodies; in the case of early years it is mainly Ofsted. In this way we can see that this is a lengthy process and legislation can be the end result of 'taking the temperature' of popular opinion and society's thinking, and not the beginning of the process of sparking those discussions regarding society's rights and responsibilities.

In order to be at the forefront of legislation and not just complying with it, we would ask you to think about the step forward that an early years setting needs to take in order to be a shaper of future legislation and a leader of forward thinking in terms of gender and the way that girls and boys grow up to be men and women.

Legislation is not just about words on paper. It is the legal enshrinement of principles that should guide and underpin early years practice in daycare settings. It is important for practitioners to discuss their own moral compass in relation to Acts of Parliament. Ideas about gender can be an integral part of a person's way of being and attitudes can be, sometimes unconsciously, passed to children. 'Boys don't cry', 'Mummies look after the babies', 'the car table is the boys' corner'. All of these comments are not in the spirit of a legislation that promotes equality and diversity. Caring for children can unlock ideas about parenting that we have had since a very early age and don't always realise. This can be a positive aspect, for example, singing a long forgotten nursery rhyme or poem. In the matter of attitudes though this can be an outdated idea that is no longer relevant in terms of a setting's legal duty and it is important that a staff team conduct an audit of these kinds of attitudes during trainings and meetings and any such statements are challenged.

We refer to this self-auditing of values throughout the book but here we give it more emphasis by setting it against a legal obligation as well as a moral one. Good equalities practice is not an added extra that can be chosen or not, but an integral part of the curriculum in all areas of the UK. We have examined all four curriculums of the nation states and it is clear that in some there are stronger statements about diversity than in others. Ultimately though it is a base line of all of the different guidance that all children need to be treated with respect and their opinions and choices should be given serious consideration. We hope that we have been able to make it clear that gender is an important element in any good equalities practice. As such it has to be carried out and as part of being a professional early years worker we need to look carefully at our attitudes to gender in order to ensure that we are meeting our legal obligations and providing the best service to the children we care for. We also need to support and respect the rights of the adults who work with the children and ensure that they are protected against discriminatory actions in the workplace. In this way adults and children can thrive in an environment that meets their emotional, developmental and statutory needs.

References

ACAS (2011) *The Equality Act 2010* [Online]. Available at http://m.acas.org.uk/ index.aspx?articleid=3017 (accessed 18 August 2015).

Department for Education (2014) *Early Years Foundation Stage 2014* [Online]. Available at www.foundationyears.org.uk/files/2014/07/EYFS_framework_ from_1_September_2014__with_clarification_note.pdf (accessed 19 August 2015).

Early Education (2012) *Development Matters in the Early Years Foundation Stage* [Online]. Available at https://early-education.org.uk/sites/default/ files/Development%20Matters%20in%20the%20Early%20Years%20 Foundation%20Stage%20-%20FINAL.pdf (accessed 7 December 2015).

Early Years Foundation Stage (2014) *Guidance on the Standards that School and Childcare Providers Must Meet for the Learning, Development and Care of Children Under 5* [Online]. Available at www.gov.uk/government/ publications/early-years-foundation-stage-framework—2 (accessed 2 October 2015).

Education Scotland (2015a) *Pre-Birth to Three: Positive Outcomes for Scotland's Children and Families* [Online]. Available at www.educationscotland.gov.uk/ learningandteaching/earlylearningandchildcare/prebirthtothree/national guidance/index.asp (accessed 24 August 2015).

Education Scotland (2015b) *The Purpose of the Curriculum* [Online]. Available at www.educationscotland.gov.uk/learningandteaching/thecurriculum/what iscurriculumforexcellence/thepurposeofthecurriculum/index.asp (accessed 24 August 2015).

Equality and Human Rights Commission (2015) *Creating a Fairer Britain* [Online]. Available at www.equalityhumanrights.com/private-and-public-sector-guidance/guidance-all/faqs (accessed 19 August 2015).

Manchester Metropolitan University (2015) *The Women's Timeline* [Online]. Available at www.mmu.ac.uk/equality-and-diversity/doc/gender-equality-timeline.pdf (accessed 18 August 2015).

Morris, N. (2015) *Gender Pay Gap: Firms Who Pay Men More Than Women to Be 'Named and Shamed'* [Online]. Available at www.independent.co.uk/ news/uk/politics/firms-who-pay-men-more-than-women-to-be-named-and-shamed-10386383.html (accessed 19 August 2015).

Northern Ireland Department of Education (2012) *Curriculum Guidance for Pre School Education* [Online]. Available at http://beta.ccea.org.uk/sites/ default/files/docs/curriculum/pre_school/preschool_guidance.pdf (accessed 24 August 2015).

Ofsted (2015) *Early Years Inspection Handbook* [Online]. Available at www.gov.uk/government/publications/inspecting-early-years-handbook-for-inspectors (accessed 24 August 2015).

Price, D. and Ota, C. (2014) *Leading and Supporting Early Years Teams*. Oxon: Routledge.

Price, D. and Tayler, K. (2015) *LGBT Diversity and Inclusion in Early Years Education*. Oxon: Routledge.

Spencer, H. (2015) *Gender Pay Gap Means Female Bosses In The UK Are Working 100 Minutes A Day 'For Free'* [Online]. Available at www.graziadaily.co.uk/2015/08/gender-pay-gap-means-female-bosses-in-the-uk-are-working-100-minutes-a-day-for-free (accessed 25 August 2015).

United Nations (1981) *Convention on the Elimination of All Forms of Discrimination against Women* [Online]. Available at https://treaties.un.org/Pages/showDetails.aspx?objid=080000028000309d and www.ohchr.org/en/hrbodies/cedaw/pages/cedawindex.aspx (accessed 18 August 2015).

Welsh Government (2015) *Foundation Stage Profile* [Online]. Available at http://gov.wales/topics/educationandskills/earlyyearshome/foundation-phase/foundation-phase-profile/?lang=en (accessed 24 August 2015).

4 Working with families

This chapter can be read in conjunction with two other chapters in this book as it refers to Chapter 6 where we look at the role of the leader and manager in working with families who may have concerns about male workers in the setting. There are also links to Chapter 3 where we examine the legislation that frames the work of the setting and where it relates to equalities and our legal duties.

Ideas about gender

We start with this quote from Meg March to her sister Jo in the children's book *Little Women*. Meg is at her wits' end with her younger sister's 'tomboyish' behaviour. As people who grew up with this book we admired Jo's rebellious spirit and refusal to accept the norms that society demanded from her – norms that were even more rigid than those that girls may face today in the UK:

> You are old enough to leave off boyish tricks and behave better, Josephine. It didn't matter so much when you were a little girl; but now you are so tall, and turn up your hair you should remember that you are a young lady.
>
> (Alcott 1994 [1868]: 7)

We use this chapter to look at ideas about gender generally and how thinking has changed since the days of *Little Women*. We do this in the context of supporting parents as well as the other adults who we come into contact with in the setting – carers, staff members and other agencies – all of whom have their own ideas about gender, as in what is a man and a woman and what is their role. These ideas come from life experiences and upbringing. Because they can be rooted in the adult's childhood they can be out of step with current thinking, and current thinking can also shed a new light on the past.

> From the writings of Shakespeare (*Twelfth Night, Much Ado about Nothing*); Mark Twain; Louisa May Alcott; and contemporary characters in literature that include Scout in *To Kill a Mockingbird*; Frankie turning into Francis in *Member of the Wedding*; Pippi Longstocking, who is full of phallic exuberance; and Smidge, the sensitive boy with strong maternal instincts, writers throughout the centuries have articulated the theme of gender role fluidity. Homosexual behavior and role reversal cross-dressing are as old as recorded history.
>
> (Crompton 2006 cited in Knight 2014: 58)

In Knight's paper (2014) she discusses the natural gender fluidity that children have when they are young. You might have seen this in your practice in the way that boys and girls play with a selection of toys and exhibit a range of behaviours. However, this fluidity is only in opposition to the more binary notions of gender that adults may possess. By this we mean the idea that 'boys do this and behave in this way' and 'girls do this and behave in this way'. If that is what we believe and we are rigid about it then any deviation from what we perceive as the norm is seen as breaking the boundaries, for instance behaving as a 'tomboy' or being 'effeminate'. However, if we view gender on a spectrum with very stereotypical definitions of masculinity and femininity at each end but then a whole range of other possibilities as well then we don't see fluidity as anything other than normal.

What we are saying here is that people and children demonstrate a range of behaviours and that can change over time and also within contexts. Notions of what is male and what is female shouldn't confine these behaviours. We can see that clearly in young children, as boys might play with trucks and cars one day and glitter and feathers the next. We would only see this as noteworthy if we think of glitter and feathers as 'girly' and trucks and cars as 'boys' toys'.

The fact is that some boys and girls are on either end of the spectrum in terms of what choices they make and other children are at different points of the spectrum and move up and down the full length of their options. There are many different ways to be a man and a woman and we should allow children the option to explore all of these ways.

The whole concept of gender as socially rather than biologically constructed is an issue that we have as a theme running through this book, especially in Chapter 2, and is unpicked in much greater detail in a range of books and articles that are listed in this book. (See the list in Appendix 2.) It is very much a live issue that underpins so many aspects of society. We can see that in any shop we go into where boys' clothes and toys are in certain colours and cover certain 'masculine' topics and girls do the same. In fact there are very few resources for children that are marketed as gender neutral. Now we could say that children tend to choose things that are at the point in the gender spectrum that they feel most comfortable in but we could also discuss whether these choices are manipulated by society and the expectations of the adults around them. Some children will not conform to those roles and expectations that society has of them.

The two basic arguments that are examined in Knight's (2014) paper are: firstly, that children should be supported in deciding which gender they most align with, that may be different from the one that they were assigned at birth. Secondly, that gender is socially constructed and we should be able to live in a state of fluid gender where we can take from whichever gender whatever we choose at any given time.

We would just remind you again that there are many different ways to be a man or a woman and that the way that children choose may not fit into the preconceived ideas of the adults around them as to what that should be. Our work in a setting is to empower children to make those choices as freely as they can and have those explorations and also to support parents and carers when this challenges their own ideas. We look in Chapter 6 at talking to a male carer when his son is choosing 'girly' clothes in the dressing-up area and he is not happy with that choice. We suggest that having a clear statement about diversity and the wide-ranging aspects of gender is an important starting point when having these discussions with parents and carers about situations like this.

In this chapter we look at gender in terms of supporting families and adults who may have different views from those that are held as part of the setting's ethos. We also look at ways that we can challenge those views and so support the children that we care for.

Case study 4.1

Working with families

We start this section by looking at a case study where the family and the child needed support with issues of gender. This case study has been kindly shared with us – we would like to name the person but for the purposes of anonymising this case study and respecting the privacy of the family and setting we are unable to; they know who they are and they have our thanks for their assistance and generosity in sharing this reflective piece. The case study is told in the voice of the practitioner and is unedited from their actual words.

One of the children I support in my Year 2 class is a transgender child. Although physically a boy, she does not feel comfortable with her pronoun. The child's parents sought professional support and requested that our school supports the desired social transition. In order to be able to provide the appropriate support the child required, I received transgender training alongside other members of staff, prior to the transition. Transitions are categorised in social and medical. The social transition I am currently supporting includes change of pronoun from he to she, change of clothes and change of name as well as toilet facilities.

I felt quite anxious on the first day back to school, as this was Frank's first day at school as Summer. Our first task was to introduce this concept to the whole class in a PHSE session. This was not a task that we could prepare for, as there was no way of knowing how the children would react.

One of the boys came up to me very excited and said 'Oh my days Mrs Thornton, you won't believe what happened in the holidays? I think Frank has turned into a girl!' Summer arrived seconds later before I could respond, in her skirt and pigtails. I greeted her with a big smile saying 'Good morning Summer, did you have a nice holiday?' She just beamed at me with the biggest smile I had ever seen. Frank had always been a quiet, sad looking boy who would often choose to play alone. Summer on the other hand was surrounded by girls and everyone seemed to want to be her new best friend.

The class teacher introduced the concept and importance of tolerance with reference to lunch boxes, toys, faith, skin colour after which she mentioned that Frank did not feel happy being Frank and that she feels happier being Summer. One of the boys replied that his Dad said that it is not normal, that he must have like a sickness in his head or something! I felt shocked by this comment, as this was exactly the kind of comments I had feared. The class teacher very calmly but firmly explained that we are all different and if Frank felt happier as Summer that it was everyone's responsibility to respect and support her decision. The same child then in full agreement announced that he himself had a new name too. All the children readily accepted Summer's social transition! I focused on using Summer's name as well as the correct pronoun each time I addressed her and ensured that the children were doing the same.

Points to consider

* What would you have done in this situation? What would have been your worries and fears?

- This child is in KS1 and so not in the early years age range – do you think this makes a difference and if so why?

- If you had further training what do you think it should cover?

- What do you think are the main issues?

- What other responses might you encounter from other children, practitioners and parents?

Discussion

Below are the reflective points that emerged from the practitioner's point of view. They had been thinking about the very issues that we highlight above and this is their response, again unedited and in their words:

> I cannot remember the last time that I felt this much out of my comfort zone. I had only ever seen a trans-person in the supermarket before and never gave the subject matter much thought. A testimony to my own ignorance. The training itself opened my eyes to a world I was not even aware that existed.
>
> I was overwhelmed at the amount of prejudice out there and the realisation that it was my responsibility to protect Summer from this within the school environment.
>
> Having been bullied most of my school life, I expected the worst of the children. Before the session I had various scenarios going through my head of children laughing at Summer and making insensitive comments. The one negative comment that was made was a child parroting their parent seeking answers. When my inner anger faded I realised that it is within my power to make a difference. It was strange at first calling Frank Summer and using a different pronoun. I was really worried that I would get it wrong and that Summer would be upset. Now I do not even think about it and just enjoy working with a happy little girl.

> ### *Points to consider from the reflection above*
>
> * Does anything from this honest piece of writing resonate with you?
>
> * Can you see how a practitioner's own experiences can affect their practice?
>
> As practitioners it is our duty to comply with the Equality Act 2010 and the Human Rights Act and create a safe environment for the children in our care. The Equality Act 2010 protects not only from discriminating behaviour on grounds of age, disability, race, religion or belief. It also protects gender reassignment. We may not come across gender reassignment in children very often but in order to prevent transphobia it is vital that all practitioners develop an understanding of trans issues.

Discussion on transgender

We have used this case study as we felt that it raised some very interesting points. Firstly it challenges the 'comfort zone' that the practitioner refers to. They talk about having only seen a person who is transgendered in a supermarket and never thinking that it would be part of their own experience. If we provide a service to children and families then we are including all children and families and it is possible that some of their experiences will be very different from ours.

In terms of gender then this experience is one that could be outside anything that you have explored in your work unless you have personal experience of transgender issues or are close to someone who has. In order to fully provide an inclusive and enabling environment where we work in partnership with parents there can be challenges.

We believe that it is imperative that, as practitioners providing that support, we constantly audit our own feelings, views, opinions and ask ourselves where they have come from. Are they fact, opinion or are they a product of our own experiences and upbringing and bear no relation to the reality of what is happening now?

Activity

This is a useful activity to do in a staff meeting. It's a team building activity but also leads to some reflective and thoughtful outcomes if it is followed by a discussion. Firstly, divide the whole group into twos and ask them to answer a series of questions about each other – *without asking each other the answers*. They need to be able to see the questions and also have a pen and paper in order to write their answers down. We suggest about ten questions, for example:

- What is this person's favourite colour?
- What is their favourite thing to eat?
- Where would they ideally like to go on holiday?
- Who was their teenage idol?
- What do they watch on TV?
- What would they drink on a night out?
- What kind of music do they listen to?
- What kind of films does this person like?
- What did they want to be when they grew up?
- If it's raining, do they use an umbrella or a raincoat?

In answering these questions practitioners have to: guess, make assumptions, look at the person and think about them, draw on their previous knowledge of them – anything but actually ask them.

Reflective points

- How many did people get right?
- How did they reach the answers they put?

This is a fun activity to do, especially with a group of people who think that they know each other. What is a learning point at the end of it is that many of the answers we put were not based on fact but on guesswork. Taking that into our wider life we can see that in reaching judgements we often make assumptions about each other and that is a process that is perhaps inevitable as we have so much information to process that we are inclined to link it to something else that we know. However, when working with families and offering a public service that is framed by legal duty, we have to ensure that we are not carrying out actions that affect those families which are informed by assumptions rather than by reality.

Making assumptions

In case study 4.1 above, the practitioner was influenced by their own experience and memories of what had happened to them as a child and realised how strong an influence this could be on their actions.

This is excellent reflective thinking of a level that should be constantly feeding and influencing our practice as it ensures that we are interacting with families in a way that is rooted in the reality of what is happening and not dominated by assumptions and our own history.

It might be that when reflecting on case study 4.1 you could have considered the fact that it focuses on a child from Year 2, and yet in this book we are looking at children in the early years foundation stage. As a result you might have concluded that this issue could not be part of your own practice as the children that you work with would be too young to be affected by this. In order to challenge this idea we look at extracts from this recent article in *The Guardian* (12 September 2015).

Case study 4.2

Cassie Wilson can pinpoint the moment her daughter Melanie became her son, Tom. They were in the supermarket and Melanie, then two and a half, said: 'I don't want to be a girl any more – I'm going to be a boy, and I'm going to be called Tom.'

'That was that,' Cassie tells me. 'I said: "Come on, then, Tom." He could have said he was called anything and I would have thought, great, fine, let's get on with the shop.'

'I was wearing my Spiderman costume,' Tom, now five, remembers.

'Yes, you were,' Cassie nods.

But it didn't end when they left the shop. 'The next day, when Tom woke up, I said: "Morning, Melanie" and he said: "I told you yesterday! My name is Tom!" It just went on from there.'

(Kleeman 2015)

The article goes on:

Cassie says she knows that Tom is very young to be transgender, but he is just one of a striking number of children who have been referred to the Tavistock and Portman NHS Trust's Gender Identity Development Service in London over the past five years. A multidisciplinary clinic where all British transgender children are assessed, the service has seen referrals increase by 50% every year, from 97 new cases in 2009 to 697 in 2014. Young children such as Tom are unusual, but not rare: last year alone, close to 100 of those referred were aged 10 or younger.

(Kleeman 2015)

Points to consider

* Were you surprised by the age of the child in this case study and the figures above?

- Does this change your thinking about the first case study at all?

- Would you feel prepared to support this child and their family in your setting?

- If not, what do you think that you need to do?

- Can you think of any reason why numbers have increased?

Discussion

We hope that you can see that it is possible that a child similar to the one above might be already present at your setting. We would also say that, in terms of staff discussions and training, it is better not to wait until an issue like the one in the case study reveals itself but to have thought this through as a team. In this way if a child like Tom is in your setting then you will feel better prepared and able to support both him and his family.

Share as a team what you feel about this – are there any viewpoints that staff members hold that might get in the way of giving someone like Tom and his family your complete support? If there are then it would be good to talk them through now rather than when you are attempting to move forward with the situation. We would suggest liaising with the training section of the appropriate local authority in order to set up some transgender awareness training with a suitably experienced person in order to make sure that the team has the correct level of skills and awareness in order to meet any challenges that may arise. This training may seem specialised and it may be that you will not need to use the specifics of it. We would suggest that having any training like this moves you forward as a team in terms of openness and honesty with each other. It also enables you to more fully support the diverse range of families and children who come to your setting. It will also help you and your team to be open with children who may not identify as trans, but who may be exploring or challenging their own gender and stereotypes around that as we have discussed.

Supporting families

In addition to supporting families who have children who are exploring a range of ways of expressing gender it may be that practitioners need to support parents who are going through the same process. It might be that a father or mother who you have contact with at the setting either talks to you in advance about their wish to be known as different from their current identity, or that they just come to the setting and present as their new identity, and you have to assimilate this information and support them, their child and the other children and staff in the setting.

Case study 4.3

Steve is the father of a child who is one of your key children in a nursery. You work in the toddler room and the child, Lucy, is two years old. Lucy's mother works long hours and it is mainly Steve who drops Lucy off and picks her up. You have a good relationship with Steve and he often talks to you about Lucy's progress and things that she has done or said at home. The setting is closed over the summer and when you return Lucy's mother Michelle brings Lucy to the setting. Michelle is very agitated and after she has settled Lucy in she pulls you to one side and tells you that Steve is transitioning. She is tearful and upset and you take her to the interview room and try and calm her down. She tells you that Steve is a 'freak' and that she doesn't want him to drop Lucy off or pick her up because she doesn't want the other parents or children to know. However, because of her work she can't see an alternative and is distraught.

Steve is living in the family home and they are going to family therapy and trying to keep the family together as they have two older children as well. The next day Steve comes to the nursery as usual with Lucy and he is wearing a dress and wig and makeup. The other parents that are dropping their children off stop chatting outside the building and scatter, looking at each other and smiling. The children in the nursery take no notice of Steve but you see the other staff in the room staring and one of them laughs with another staff member. You are unsure what to do.

Points to consider

- What are you going to say to Steve?
- What are you going to say to Lucy?
- Will you speak to the other staff?
- Will you speak to the other parents?

Discussion

(Note that in some of this discussion we are using 'they' and 'their' to avoid a male or female pronoun.)

We have no prescriptive answers for what is a sensitive situation. What we would say firstly is that there needs to be reflective thinking and discussion with your line manager and that careful thought must be given to avoid taking any hasty actions.

What we would also say is that there needs to be an immediate and supportive response to Steve as they are there and the moment has to be handled whereas other actions can wait until later. We would suggest that if Steve has time then it would be good to talk to them in a private place. If they have to rush off then a smile and 'good to see you – what would you like us to call you from now on?' will be a holding action and show Steve that you want to communicate with them in a positive and encouraging way and are able to acknowledge the situation without any difficulty.

Once Steve has told you what they want to be called then you can go to your manager and ask them to let the whole staff team know that Steve is now known as Melissa and wants to be referred to by the female pronoun. You can then have a discussion with your room staff to ensure that they will not react in an inappropriate manner again.

Room colleagues and staff members

We would suggest that it is best not to chastise your room colleagues as moving people on from their views is not effectively done in anger. We hope that this chapter has shown you that such views are often the result of one's own parenting and upbringing and need to be carefully dealt with. We would suggest that you need to organise a time when the children aren't there to have a meeting to talk the issue through.

We would hope that the setting has an ethos of openness around discussing gender issues (as well as other issues – see Chapter 6). In this arena a frank talk where staff members can say what they find challenging about the situation without feeling that they will be ridiculed or 'told off' we hope will lead to an honest and respectful engagement where the staff can work as a united team in order to support the family no matter what their own views are.

It might be that staff members have a belief from their faith or cultural background that makes it difficult for them to see such issues in a positive way. We would suggest that, while sympathetic to their difficulties, they are working in a service that is open to the public in all of their diversity. They also have their work framed by legislation and part of that is to support and welcome children and families whatever their background. Again, we cannot stress enough the importance of a clear vision statement here. All staff and families need to understand that by working or engaging with the setting, they are also upholding and agreeing with the setting's vision statement and thus its ethos.

In terms of the other staff in the setting, they are the responsibility of the manager – although we would certainly say that any derogatory remarks in the staff room made in your earshot need to be challenged by you.

Lucy

We would suggest that, in order to support Lucy, you need to ensure that she has lots of opportunity to talk to you if she wishes to, for instance in the home play area, through reading books – set out those that are relevant to her that might prompt her to talk to you, and with activities like Duplo figures.

Ask her parents what they want you to do if you carry out activities like making 'Mother's Day' cards. We would suggest that this level of sensitivity would be a matter of course with any child who needs extra support in terms of the situation that they have with their mother, for example if a child has two mothers or doesn't have a mother. As an aside here we would always recommend saying to a child 'Where's your grown up', rather than 'Where's your mummy/daddy' as we don't always know who cares for that child. In the case of the setting we would hope that you would know who their parent or carer was, but it is still good practice.

Parents and carers

Finally we need to consider your dealings with the parents who use the setting and feature in the case study. We would suggest that you lead by example and make sure that they see that you are treating Melissa with respect and acting in the way that she wants you to in terms of recognising her as a woman. We would suggest that you stress this and make a point of it, at first anyway. If any of the parents take the initiative and talk to you about her then that is a different matter and you would be able to have a direct discussion with them. It might be that your manager, after talking to Melissa, would think it appropriate to send a note out to the other parents in the class but that would be after discussion. If such a note were sent then you would need to make yourself available for any discussion that might come up as a result.

We also need to discuss the possibility of the nursery having a staff member who is trans. We hope that you see that the basic ideas of good practice would apply here as well in terms of support and relations with other staff members and parents. We would also refer you to *LGBT Diversity and Inclusion in Early Years Education* (Price and Tayler 2015) where we refer to this issue, especially in Chapter 6.

Conclusion

We hope that this section has challenged and also informed your practice in terms of gender and children who identify as other than their birth assigned gender. We hope that you can see that supporting and communicating with families and children in this situation needs a level of sympathetic and sensitive interaction that is hard to achieve if the practitioner has deeply rooted assumptions and prejudices that they haven't examined. We would also stress the importance of having good quality training in this area so that, as a setting, you feel confident and ready to deal with this type of situation if it happened. You have no way of knowing if it might not reveal itself tomorrow. In the scenarios we detailed above there was no run up to the issue so we would suggest that it could easily be your setting which found itself in this situation.

Along with outside training we also think that making time for honest and respectful discussions as a staff team would help this process and also be part of establishing an ethos in the setting that welcomes diversity and sees it as a challenge perhaps but not as a problem.

We leave the last word to Jo March from *Little Women*:

I ain't! And if turning up my hair makes me one, I'll wear it in two tails till I'm twenty . . . I hate to think I've got to grow up and be Miss March and wear long gowns . . . it's bad enough to be a girl anyway when I like boys' games and work and manners. I can't get over my disappointment in not being a boy.

(Alcott 1994 [1868]: 4)

References

Alcott, L. (1994 [1868]) *Little Women*. Oxford: Oxford University Press.

Kleeman, J. (2015) *Transgender Children: This Is Who He Is – I Have to Respect That* [Online]. Available at www.theguardian.com/society/2015/sep/12/transgender-children-have-to-respect-who-he-is (accessed 16 September 2015).

Knight, R. (2014) Free to be you and me: normal gender-role fluidity – commentary on Diane Ehrensaft's 'listening and learning from gender-nonconforming children'. *The Psychoanalytic Study of the Child,* 68, 57–70. Available at www.psotc.com/transgender.pdf (accessed 21 September 2015).

Price, D. and Tayler, K. (2015) *LGBT Diversity and Inclusion in Early Years Education*. Oxon: Routledge.

Tavistock and Portman NHS Trust (2015) Gender Identity Development Service [Online]. Available at http://tavistockandportman.uk/care-and-treatment/information-parents-and-carers/our-clinical-services/gender-identity-development (accessed 8 December 2015).

5 | **Working with children**

The idea of working for gender equality will not be new to many early years practitioners. No one would think it good practice to base our work with young children on ideas about 'pretty little girls' and 'big strong boys'. While it is generally accepted that we should be giving boys and girls a range of opportunities to be kind, thoughtful, strong, adventurous, emotional, brave, gentle, resilient, assertive, active and nurturing, it is harder to think about how we might achieve this. What approach should we take to dealing with how children play and relate to each other and to practitioners? Should we operate a system where we provide a wide range of activities and allow children to choose freely or should we be more proactive in challenging the choices and behaviour that children express?

Activity

Think about the way the children in your setting play and the way the adults (practitioners and parents) respond to this. Look at the scenarios below. How would you respond?

- A boy was playing with dolls when his father arrived to pick him up. He said, 'Oh my word, what are we going to do with him? What is he going to be when he's older?'

- One practitioner said to another, 'Football doesn't happen in my house because I've only got girls'.

- A boy said to another boy, 'You can be the king'. The boy replied, 'No I'm a queen, there's not going to be a king'.

- When being read *Amazing Grace* (Hoffman 2007), a boy said 'Boys can't wear tutus'.

- A girl in the role-play area said to a boy, 'You can't play in here, it's for girls'.

- Some new equipment arrives at a setting. A girl is very excited about a new train set and asks if she can play with it. Some other girls laugh at her.

Discussion

In a busy, active setting it can be easy to miss exchanges between children or adults such as the ones above. Looking out for, and thinking about how to respond to, such exchanges is a challenge but is part of the commitment to providing a fully inclusive setting. In the first example, a practitioner responded by saying 'A dad?' The father replied, 'Yeah, I guess I didn't think of it like that'. A small challenge such as this can start a dialogue and can have a lasting impact on all concerned. If in the child's earshot, it also conveys a message that his play choices are valid and that the setting is a safe place for him to explore different roles.

What responses can you think of to the other scenarios that might have a similar impact? You may like to use this as a discussion point in your staff team. Try putting some of the responses into practice and then revisit them in future team meetings or discuss them with a colleague.

What might good practice look like?

Case study 5.1

One World Nursery is registered for 35 children and operates as part of Brighton University. Initially set up to provide childcare for the children of staff and students, it is now open to the local community. They have a team of 14 practitioners working full- and part-time and whose qualifications range from Level 3 to EYPS with one member of staff studying for an MA in Education (Early Years). One of the Deputy Mangers also has a Montessori diploma. Of the 14 practitioners, one is male.

They are housed in a large converted barn with a multi-purpose space where they start and end the day, an art room and the 'rainbow room' where the children have table-top activities, eat their lunch and where they sleep. There is also an additional room used for storage of resources and where they offer small group activities. They have a large garden on different levels. They have just secured funding to have further work done to the garden that will include the opening up of the art room to the garden to enable free-flow and the addition of a mud kitchen.

Their *Nursery Handbook* states that they aim to 'provide an anti-bias learning environment, which is safe, stimulating and monitored to meet the needs of all' (University of Brighton 2014: 4). One of their guiding principles is that:

> Children will not be excluded or disadvantaged because of ethnicity, culture or religion, home background, special educational needs, disability, gender or ability. All children are shown respect and treated as individuals.
>
> (University of Brighton 2014: 4)

Their Equality of Opportunity Policy in the handbook says that the nursery staff:

> recognise the important role they play in promoting the understanding of, and having a commitment to, the principles of equality and freedom from discrimination on the grounds of nationality, religion, culture, race, gender, sexuality, physical ability, marital and parental status, health, social class, language or race. We are committed to providing a loving and positive

learning environment, free from prejudice, discrimination and fear, in which all children, their families and the staff feel accepted, respected and valued.

(University of Brighton 2014: 32)

Amongst other ways, they aim to do this by:

- Acting as positive role models ourselves. Monitoring our actions and language in regard to working with all the children, parents/carers, visitors, other professionals and each other.
- Responding to (and challenging) discriminatory behaviour/remarks appropriately.
- Carefully selecting resources that give the children (and others) a balanced view of the world.
- Providing materials that help children to develop their self-respect and to respect others, and by avoiding stereotypes and derogatory picture messages or words about any individual or group.
- Reflecting on our current practice and continuing to update and increase our knowledge around equalities issues.

(University of Brighton 2014: 32–33)

The nursery has a named equalities representative who has taken part in local authority equalities training. The nursery follows all Equal Opportunities guidance provided by the university and all relevant equalities legislation.

They are greatly committed to challenging gender inequality and to providing equal opportunities to girls and boys to explore a wide range of activities and experiences. They constantly question their own assumptions and the ways in which they may inadvertently treat girls and boys differently. As one practitioner explained:

We live in such a hugely gendered society that if we weren't treating them differently in some way it would be a miracle.

I mean, given the influences on us, the influences on them and the way that people conform to expected norms, I think that you have to make a real, real conscious effort one hundred percent of the time to be able to step right outside of that and be completely gender neutral.

As well as trying to remain aware of their own assumptions, they are also clear that the children in their setting have already had many experiences before they come to the setting and that these experiences continue outside the setting throughout their time with them. They are committed to providing the care and education that fits with their own philosophy without undermining anything that may happen differently at home or elsewhere.

Some of the ways they see as important in trying to achieve this are as follows:

- Making a variety of choices themselves, for example, what they wear, how they engage with activities and the choices they make in relation to this. This often evokes interesting conversations with the children.

- These conversations are an important part of the process and help create the ethos of the setting.

- This ethos contributes to giving children the freedom to play in a range of ways, for example, boys exploring the dressing-up clothes with a greater sense of choice.

- When choices such as this are explored by children, they are never made fun of or met with jokey comments. Any comments from other children are dealt with through discussion and exploration using a sustained shared thinking approach.

- There needs to be the confidence within a staff team to explore ideas and to have discussions about things that can sometimes be uncomfortable.

- There is a need to be aware of the links with other forms of discrimination (intersectionality) and that experiences of race, culture and class are additional factors that impact on experiences of gender. There is a need to be respectful of these differences.

- All resources and equipment need to be regularly reviewed and refreshed and new ideas need to be acted upon.

Points to consider

- What does your equalities policy look like?

- Do you discuss gender in your team, with parents and with the children?

- Do you provide a range of equipment and resources that allow children to explore different roles?

- Do you provide positive role models?

- Do you reflect on, discuss and update your policy and practice?

- Do you feel confident about challenging discriminatory remarks, whether from a child, a parent or another member of staff?

- Are assumptions made (by staff, parents or children) about how male and female practitioners will act within the setting?

Discussion

Although the requirements to have an equalities policy are no longer part of the EYFS, settings are still required to adhere to all equalities legislation (see Chapter 3 for a full discussion of relevant legislation) and developing a clear policy can help think this through. Discussing gender in the staff team will help flesh out thoughts about your ethos and how you want to approach the challenges that can occur.

> While resources, equipment and activities are a crucial part of your provision, your ethos and willingness to challenge yourself and to think in a reflective way is of equal importance.

War, weapon and superhero play

Many practitioners will be familiar with play that involves themes of war and weapons and with superhero play. Often it will mainly be boys that engage with this type of play and practitioners will have to consider how they want to approach this, whether to support it and engage with it or whether they want to adopt a zero tolerance to play of this kind. While settings would be very unlikely to provide ready-made toy weapons it would be an unusual setting that has not had to think about how to deal with children making guns out of construction kits or using other materials to aid their war, weapon and superhero play.

Holland (2003) has extensively researched war, weapon and superhero play and came to the conclusion that all children benefited from relaxing the zero tolerance approach. She argues that this type of play is almost exclusively associated with boys and that they are very persistent in their attempts to engage with play of this kind, meaning that practitioners spend a lot of time trying to curb and control it.

This intolerance towards war, weapon and superhero play has a long history dating back to the 1970s and to the assumption that play of this kind imitates the same power relations as those involved with the use of real weapons. The fact that play of this kind is largely engaged with by boys confirmed this view that it was a mirror image of adult power relations between men and women. There were assumed to be links with male violence towards women and that the best approach was to clearly and categorically state that 'We don't play with guns here' (Holland 2003). The very active peace movement at this time was also a large contributing factor with many practitioners feeling uncomfortable supporting children engaging in this kind of play. While there is little evidence of any policy that stated that this was how practice should be, it was very widespread.

The concern with war, weapon and superhero play has shifted from banning it because it might cause violence to thinking about the impact on boys' self-esteem if their play choices are never validated. If boys are constantly getting the message that we don't like the way they play, are they also getting the message that we don't like them? Holland concludes:

> Whatever combination of biology and social construction (nature and nurture) gives rise to the preference shown by some boys for war, weapon and superhero play and/or other forms of active and noisy play, practitioners have a professional responsibility to work with those boys and their play in a way which does not generate low self-esteem or negative gender identity.
>
> (Holland 2003: 24)

Holland (2003) suggests that, far from discouraging this kind of play or encouraging boys to engage in a wider range of play, the zero tolerance approach entrenched boys' views of themselves as male and as 'different' from girls. Practitioner concern with policing war, weapon and superhero play also says something about the play of girls and conveys the message that we are not nearly so concerned about what they are getting up to, as long as they remain quiet and passive and play nicely in the home corner.

What Holland's research tells us is that when rules around war, weapon and superhero play are relaxed, both boys and girls benefit. When boys felt supported in their play choices, there was more evidence of play that challenged gender stereotypes, for example, using a wider range of dressing-up clothes. The knock on effect for girls was that they saw a wider range of construction and role-play being supported by practitioners and this encouraged them to become more engaged. This enabled them to see engaging in a wider range of activities as being a normal and acceptable part of being a girl.

When these activities are seen solely as the preserve of boys, girls who engage in them are often labelled 'tomboys', the implication of which is that they have relinquished their girlhood. However, Martin (2011) points out that even when both boys and girls engage in superhero play there are differences and that we need to be mindful of this in how we respond. She suggests that for girls, superhero play is often about endurance and kindness rather than strength and physicality. She argues that changing practice so that both boys and girls engage in superhero play is not the end of the story and that girls need alternative stories 'that include a range of sexualities and gender positions' (Martin 2011: 128). Browne also highlights the differences between boys and girls when they engage in superhero play and suggests that: 'Male heroes and superheroes seem to encapsulate the essential characteristics of unambiguous and traditional "masculinity", while heroines, despite their brave deeds and resourcefulness, remain essentially "feminine" in that they are kind and caring' (Browne 2004: 87).

With the relaxing of the zero tolerance approach, Holland and her colleagues found that the richness of the children's play increased and that their confidence and self-esteem were raised. This was found to be true of both boys and girls, although the work of Martin (2011) and Browne (2004) warns us to make sure we are aware of the complexities of this.

Through their war, weapon and superhero play the children also had opportunities to build on their fine motor skills and their creativity as well as their language development. There was also an increase in their ability to concentrate for longer periods of time and the levels of their involvement whilst engaged in war, weapon and superhero play increased.

What does this look like in practice?

When the practitioners at One World Nursery (see case study 5.1) became concerned that they were denying the children the right to engage in one whole area of play through their zero tolerance to war, weapon and superhero play, they decided to reconsider this and see if there was anything they could do differently. Two of the practitioners had recently completed studying for Early Years Professional Status (EYPS) and belonged to a local network. They took their ideas to their group and the discussions went from there. At that time there was funding available for their professional development. They chose to use some of this to invite Penny Holland to come and talk to them.

Following this they continued to discuss the issue amongst the team and began some informal observations of their own practice and of the children at play. They realised what a very big issue they were embarking on and that they needed to take it slowly and carefully. They decided that the best approach would be for them to undertake a piece of action research.

Action research

Action research is sometimes also known as practitioner research because it is carried out by practitioners in their setting rather than by academic researchers who come in specifically to carry out a piece of research. Early years practitioners are very well placed to conduct action research as they will be the experts in their setting and will have knowledge of the children and families they work with and of the pedagogy that underpins their practice. They will also be aware of the issues that concern them and that they wish to investigate and learn more about. The impetus for action research is often that an issue has been identified that practitioners feel needs to change in some way and the research is used as a way of exploring what changes might be needed and how they might be implemented (Roberts-Holmes 2011).

Many early years practitioners will be familiar with reflective practice and will be used to thinking about issues in this way. Staff teams often use reflective practice as a way of informing their practice and their relationships with the children, the families and with each other. Action research has links with reflective practice in that it is cyclical and involves practitioners in being open to thinking about issues in new and challenging ways.

MacNaughton et al. (2001) describe this cycle in the following way. After the issue to be researched has been identified, the researchers:

- observe;

- plan actions based on the observations;

- implement the actions;

- reflect on what happened;

- share and collaborate with others;

- build theories to guide further action.

The cycle then starts again with observations to assess the impact so far. Further actions are then planned and implemented followed by reflection, sharing and collaborating. Theories are adapted and built on. Further action is observed and the cycle continues.

The key features of action research are:

- It is a social process.
- It is participatory.
- It is practical and collaborative.
- It is emancipatory.
- It is critical.
- It is reflexive.
- It aims to transform both theory and practice.

(Kemmis and McTaggart 2005 cited in Mukherji
and Albon 2015: 116)

An important aspect of action research is to acknowledge that by being a participant, you are part of the research in a way that you would not be in a more objective approach. Your beliefs and values will be part of the process and that can influence the approach you take and the outcome you achieve. This is partly why honest and open reflection, individually and within the team, is so crucial. Walker and Solvason state that rather than claiming that you can maintain a detached objectivity it is better to say 'here I am, I am part of this work' (2014: 30).

At the time of starting their action research the practitioners at One World Nursery operated a zero tolerance approach to war, weapon and superhero play. Their response to children playing in this way was 'We don't play with guns here' or 'We don't play like that here'. By starting to unpick this approach they began to think about the significant messages they were giving to the children concerned,

- We don't like what you are doing.

- We don't value your play.

- The children were being encouraged to lie about their constructions by, for example, constructing a gun but saying it was a fishing rod.

They began their action research by continuing the informal observations they had started and then began a series of meetings and discussions within the team, with the parents and with the children. They realised that there were very strong feelings about this issue in both directions. Some staff and parents had strongly held views and political beliefs stemming from the peace and feminist movements, others felt there was nothing wrong with war, weapon and superhero play.

The next step was for the practitioners to try out re-enactments of how they might deal with a range of scenarios and what they might say to the children. Some staff felt unsure how they would approach this and that they would not be able to deal with it. They decided that initially the more confident members of staff would step in to support the less confident. Over time the confidence levels of all staff increased and now all practitioners are fully on board with the new approach.

Through their action research they highlighted some important aspects of this kind of play that now inform their practice and are reflected in their 'Superhero, weapons and war play policy' (One World Nursery 2014).

- War is part of many children's lives. For some children this will be via television or computer games. For others this will be their own lived experience and they may be living here as refugees or asylum seekers. Others will have parents or other family members in the armed forces.

- When the play is supported and allowed to develop they discovered that much of it was about empowerment rather than violence.

- It is important to set allowing this play within the context of giving the children the right and the language to say no when they do not want to take part.

- This play can be used as an opportunity to discuss and explore what it means to be a superhero or what makes an individual heroic.

- When the children have the freedom to explore without the fear of rebuke, they are freed up to play in a wider range of ways.

- By freeing some children, all children are free to try things out too resulting in more varied play.

- Resourcing this play needs to be thought about very carefully especially in relation to finding a range of superhero representations for girls and black children.

In conclusion the practitioners feel using action research as a way of considering their practice around war, weapon and superhero play has been an example of change being really well led. The team have all supported each other, the parents and the children well. They have had many conversations and not rushed the change. They avoided judgement and have made changes to their practice that they believe facilitates a very rich role-play experience for the children.

Thinking outside the box

The ways in which we think about gender and the ways in which we challenge this can still very much be informed by what we see as behaviour that conforms or challenges stereotypical gendered behaviour. It is easy to slip into simplistic thinking about this and to think that a girl who prefers playing in the home corner and a boy who prefers construction sets are conforming to gendered expectations while children who play in other ways are challenging this. Sometimes it can be useful to think in different ways and ask yourself if there is another way of looking at a situation.

Case study 5.2

Sue is an early years practitioner who works in a large daycare setting. She is room leader in the pre-school room and she has Early Years Teacher Status. She takes a leadership role throughout the setting in terms of developing practice. She is very committed to reflective practice and encourages all the practitioners to think carefully about the way they interact with the children and about the assumptions they hold about how children learn and develop. She is particularly interested in gender and in trying to avoid gender stereotyping in the way they plan for and respond to the children in the setting. Sue describes a recent activity and the thinking that followed it.

Recently I carried out an activity with a small group of children. There were both boys and girls involved and they were all three to four years old. We had an old radio that no longer worked and we decided to take it apart. We weren't trying to fix it but simply to have fun unscrewing it and looking inside, taking bits out, making guesses about how it worked or what function different parts had.

The children had small screwdrivers and small pots to put the nuts and bolts and other parts in. One of the little girls was very involved and concentrated deeply. She carefully collected the screws, even the tiniest ones, and put them in her pot. When she had a good collection she stirred them enthusiastically with her screwdriver and announced 'I makin a cake!'

My first thought was that I was failing miserably at challenging stereotypical behaviour and that whatever activities I provide for the children they will behave in fixed ways. I felt quite disheartened. I reflected on this activity after and realised that there is more than one way to respond. Initially I saw what this child was doing by equating it to imaginative role-play the same as if she was pretending to make a cake in the home corner.

I began to consider if there was another way of looking at this. I shifted my focus away from looking at the 'content' of what she was doing (pretending to make a cake) to looking at the 'form' instead. Using what I know about schemas and the work of Chris Athey (2007) I began to think about this child's play in terms of her interest in rotation and containing. As soon as I had thought about this, it all made sense. By observing her carefully I noticed these schemas in much of her play. She loved putting objects in containers. We could always rely on her when things needed tidying as she loved putting things in boxes so much! She also loved anything that rotated, including herself and her favourite song was 'Winding the bobbin up'.

My reflection led me to realise that if I had followed through on my initial thoughts about the observation I may have then planned a cake making activity. By thinking about the form instead of the content I could plan for this child at a much deeper level and not be driven by what appeared to be gendered behaviour. I felt huge relief!

Through this reflective work Sue has shown that it is possible to see the way children play in a range of ways and that our responses can move beyond responding to what might appear to be gender specific play. This enables us to move beyond seeing a little girl who in interested in making cakes to a child who is interested in rotation.

Points to consider

- Did this case study make you think about any of the children you work with?

- Did it make you stop and think about ways you have interpreted children's play and how you may have viewed this differently?

- Do you think your own experiences around gender may influence how you view the children you work with?

- Do you try to engage in reflective practice in this way so that you can challenge your initial assumptions about how children play?

- This practitioner has used her knowledge of schemas to help her think about this child. Can you think of any other ideas or theories that may support you with this?

Discussion

There are many ways of thinking about the way children play and what significance this may hold. In Chapter 2 you read about challenges to developmentally appropriate practice (DAP) and how this can give wider scope to thinking about how children learn and develop. If you see gender as socially constructed you will view the way children play very differently than if you think it is biologically driven. This case study should also help you to think about different ways of thinking about how children play and what your role could be in supporting that. Keeping an open mind will enable you to think reflectively about what you see, what it might mean and how you plan for what next steps children might benefit from.

What next?

Alongside keeping an open mind about why some children may behave and play in certain ways, it can be useful to think about specific approaches that can be beneficial in terms of challenging gendered play.

It can be useful to start with simply observing the children at play.

- What kind of play takes place throughout the day?

- Who plays with what?

- Who joins in?

- Who is left out?

- What power relations can you see?

- Who uses what spaces inside and out?

You might then like to move on to look at and think about how the practitioners in your setting intervene and relate to the children.

- Are gender stereotypes avoided by, for example, never making a request for some 'big, strong boys' to help with moving equipment?
- What do adults praise or reprimand boys and girls for? Do these comments reinforce or challenge gender stereotypes?
- Do practitioners talk to children about their play, about gender and about stereotyping?
- Do practitioners join in children's play, model a range of gender roles and encourage children to explore a variety of roles themselves?

(adapted from Martin 2011: 132)

Early years practitioners have many responsibilities and challenging gender inequality can seem of less importance than keeping children safe, thinking about their development and providing for their next steps, carrying out observations and assessments, communicating with parents and carers and the many other roles that need to be carried out on a daily basis. However, being open to thinking about all aspects of inclusion is a central and vital responsibility in all early years settings. As Brown tells us:

Educational practice based on equality and justice is good educational practice and involves developing empowering relationships built on trust, respect and an appreciation of diversity . . . We have a responsibility to support children's early learning and to help them unlearn the prejudices and discriminatory attitudes they absorb from the world around them.

(Brown 2007: 1–2)

Conclusion

This chapter has not aimed to give you fixed ways of working with young children in terms of gender equality or simply a list of ideas for challenging gender inequality. While there are specific ideas suggested, the hope is more that the chapter will have given you things to think about, ideas to discuss and an awareness that the challenge is to keep an open mind and to look for multiple ways of viewing things.

The case study from One World Nursery will have helped you to think about what practice might look like in reality. The example of the action research they undertook around war, weapon and superhero play might help you to think about what areas you might like to explore as a team and how you might go about investigating and developing an area of your practice.

The second case study gives an example of what good reflective practice can lead to and what thoughts might arise for you when you are open to thinking about children's play and their gendered behaviour in a new light.

References

Athey, C. (2007) *Extending Thought in Young Children: A Parent–Teacher Partnership.* London: Paul Chapman.

Brown, B. (2007) *Unlearning Discrimination in the Early Years.* Stoke on Trent: Trentham Books.

Browne, N. (2004) *Gender Equity in the Early Years.* Maidenhead: Open University Press.

Hoffman, M. (2007) *Amazing Grace.* London: Frances Lincoln.

Holland, P. (2003) *We Don't Play with Guns Here.* Maidenhead: Open University Press.

MacNaughton, G., Rolfe, S. and Siraj-Blatchford, I. (2001) *Doing Early Childhood Research: International Perspectives on Theory and Practice.* London: Sage.

Martin, B. (2011) *Children at Play: Learning Gender in the Early Years.* London: Trentham.

Mukherji, P. and Albon, D. (2015) *Research Methods in Early Childhood*. London: Sage.

One World Nursery (2014) *Superhero, Weapons and War Play Policy*. Brighton: One World Nursery.

Roberts-Holmes, G. (2011) *Doing Your Early Years Research Project: A Step-by-Step Guide*. London: Sage.

University of Brighton (2014) *Nursery Handbook* [Online]. Available at http://staffcentral.brighton.ac.uk/xpedio/groups/Public/documents/staffcentral/doc011872.pdf (accessed 13 July 2015).

Walker, R. and Solvason, C. (2014) *Success With Your Early Years Research Project*. London: Sage.

6 Leading and managing good practice

In this chapter we start by examining the ways that managers and leaders can provide a supportive ethos in the workplace that allows staff, parents and carers and their children to feel able to fully be themselves in terms of gender. We also specifically look at the role that managers have in supporting and leading men in the childcare workforce. We believe that encouraging men to work in the early years workforce is a positive thing. Men and women working alongside each other in a caring profession can only be beneficial for children as it shows them that bringing up the next generation is a job that women and men share equally and that it is valued by society.

Having men working in childcare brings a fully rounded portrayal of society into the setting and adds a different dynamic to the staff team. We do note that having men working alongside women in early years settings is historically a new situation and so can be a sensitive issue for some. In this chapter we think about the way that managers can respect and allay parents' and carers' fears that they might have concerning the role of men in caring for their children. We look at fears relating to sexual abuse and think of a range of strategies that protect children and all staff and how we can move forward in terms of best practice in safeguarding children and also providing a diverse workforce that reflects the world around them. In having this discussion we look at notions of 'natural' roles in childcare settings and how all staff can be empowered to work at their full potential, unencumbered by ideas about gender specific roles.

In terms of gender, as in any other aspect of equalities when working with young children, the emphasis for good practice must come from the overall ethos of the setting. By this we mean that, in order to establish a culture where gender is thought about in a sensitive and meaningful way, the leadership and management of a setting is crucial.

Good practice in gender work can exist through the actions of isolated individuals in settings, but it is hard to establish this if the ethos is not top down and part of a whole setting policy. The most effective settings have managers and leaders who establish a positive environment for children and hold staff accountable in terms of their equalities practice, and this includes gender.

In Chapter 3 where we looked at legislation, we discussed how legislative responsibility rests with all staff, not just those who manage and lead the setting. It is important that all staff understand their responsibilities in terms of legislative duties. In the same way, sensitive gender work in a setting must come from all staff and be a whole staff outlook.

The leaders and managers of a setting must be able to create a whole staff ethos and motivate the staff team to all work in a sensitive and respectful way around gender issues. In this environment staff members are personally responsible for their non-discriminatory actions in regard to gender. This is enhanced by the whole staff ethos that supports and encourages this kind of work.

In this way the setting is led from the top but individuals are given responsibility as well. In this chapter we discuss how to create this kind of setting and think about practical ways that leaders and managers can ensure that this enabling environment, staffed by reflective practitioners, can come about.

We think about starting the process with a vision statement and establishing the building blocks of good practice. We continue by discussing the ways that this practice can be managed. Good practice in gender is an ongoing process and leaders and managers need to be aware that the way that the setting thinks about gender needs to be constantly audited and monitored. As with all other aspects of equalities work there is not a 'once and for all' box that can be ticked.

Vision statements

> Having a clear vision and being able to communicate that is a feature of effective leadership. It provides a point of navigation and clear statement about what a person stands for. From this vision a leader is able to challenge others by developing and creating meaningful and relevant norms, values and expectations for their organisation.
>
> (Price and Ota 2014: 44)

We would suggest that it is essential to include reference to gender in a vision statement – even if it's not as directly as the statement above. By including gender alongside cultural diversity and additional needs, a setting is ensuring that the full gamut of good equalities practice is mentioned. A vision statement is the way that a setting opens a window on their practice to parents, carers and the outside world. When parents and carers are making a decision as to where they want to place their child or practitioners are considering where they want to apply for jobs, the vision statement is the first indication of a setting's ethos that they will see. This is especially true in current times where so much information is available on the Internet.

A vision statement also provides another function. It is a very efficient way of bringing a staff team together. The vision statement should be agreed and understood by all the staff team, in the same way that the legislation requirements need to be understood and adhered to (see Chapter 3). Having open and frank discussions about the vision statement, for example writing one together as a staff team, and also thinking about how it could be interpreted, is a good way to unpick the way that practitioners think and the ideas that they have about gender.

People who have worked alongside each other for many years might find during these discussions that they have very different ideas about an enabling environment where boys and girls can make free choices about activities and feel valued.

For example, a pre-school practitioner might feel that it is necessary to make boys and girls line up separately in order to move around the setting as it reinforces their gender and that they need that reinforcement. A staff training session would be a time to unpick this and discuss practices that divide boys and girls. In this training other ways of grouping children could be suggested. These could include: colour of their socks, what they had for breakfast, if they have a cat or a dog at home, their favourite fruit and other such ideas. In this way we are emphasising what the children have in common rather than what divides them.

Activity

An example of a vision statement could be:

Here at Little Bunnies nursery we aim to help all children realise their full potential during their time with us. We respect and support all children according to their individual needs and provide a full and diverse experience that does not limit them in terms of gender and/or cultural and family background.

Points to consider

- Examine the vision statement that your setting has and think about any words that it uses that relate to gender.

- In the vision statement above there is clear reference to the uniqueness of children and the commitment of practitioners to respect and value that uniqueness and not restrict it with their own or society's assumptions.

Discussion

Think about the audience for your vision statement and how they might be interacting with it. The vision statement gives a strong picture of who you are as a setting and the ethos that you have. The vision statement can be read 'between the lines' and assumptions made as to what kind of a setting you are and what sort of experiences and environment you will be providing for children. The vision statement is important not only because of what you put into it but also **what you leave out**.

A parent who is looking for a diverse experience for their child and an indication from you that you would be able to support a child who came from a family who had a different makeup from the perceived 'norm' would be hoping to find a clear signal in your vision statement. They would be looking for signs that this would be the kind of setting that would be able to celebrate and support their child's unique experience. Not having anything in the vision statement that provides this signal could alienate potential families from considering your setting for their child.

We would argue that it is not enough to think that this good equalities practice doesn't need to be stated as it is an unspoken understanding that the setting would be working in this way. In order to provide a supportive message to families the statement needs to be overt.

Use of a vision statement

As well as the uses we have detailed above, the vision statement has very practical applications. The vision statement is valuable when deciding between priorities – for example reorganising the nursery, making changes within the staff team, deciding where to spend money. In each case the crucial question that needs to be asked is 'Does this move us further towards or further away from our vision statement?' This is the first qualifier that needs to be considered when thinking about changes in policy and practice.

Having a vision that makes good equalities practice in gender clear is also a useful tool as it says directly to staff and families that this is where the setting is in terms of practice. If there is ever any question of this commitment then the vision statement can be used to reaffirm this and move the setting back to the core of where it needs to be.

Case study 6.1

Working with parents and carers

A male carer comes to pick his child Charlie up and sees the three-year-old boy dressing up in a dress. He takes the dress off the child and hands it to the key workers saying 'I don't want my boy wearing girls' clothes – it'll give him ideas, don't let me see it again.'

The key worker is very distressed and asks you, the manager, what she should do next time the father comes to pick the child up.

Points to consider

- How can you challenge this but still be supportive of the parent and recognise that they are the main carer for their child?

- How can you support the key worker?

Discussion

Here is a situation where the vision statement is very important. As early years practitioners we know that it is crucial to work in partnership with parents and carers and to respect their views and ideology on parenting their own children. It is also important to be clear as to the kind of environment and ethos that their child will be cared for in. The vision statement is a tool that makes this very clear and can be referred to when there is any dispute.

It is a good starting point for any discussion with a parent. The manager might start by saying 'I understand that you aren't happy with Charlie wearing certain items in the dressing-up area. You know that we have a policy that respects children's choices and doesn't make assumptions about gender. Part of this is letting them choose what activities they want to do and explore everything we have to offer. It's also our legal duty to respect a child's individuality.' There then might be a further discussion on why the parent is so upset – what is it that he is worried about? The manager might give him information on the range of activities that Charlie chooses as a matter of interest or invite him to spend some time in the nursery observing. This case study links to Chapter 7 where we discuss the use of resources.

It might be that the key worker would like to lead this discussion with the parent and in that case your role would be to support them. It's important that all staff feel empowered to have these difficult conversations with parents and that they are not just the domain of the manager.

This isn't to give any credence to his worries that are clearly around Charlie's future masculinity. We need to be clear here that we are not saying that as long as Charlie chooses some traditionally 'male' activities then that's good. It might be that Charlie spends all of his time in the nursery playing with dolls, skipping outside, dressing up in dresses and other activities that are often associated with girls. That would also be good.

What we are saying here is that it is important to be clear about the nursery's policy on gender and make a firm statement about that. It is also important to find out more about where the parent's thinking is at that point in terms of gender. What are his worries and anxieties? What is it that he fears about Charlie's choices? In order to work in partnership with this parent we need to try and move him forward from his position in order to make the experience of Charlie being at the nursery happy and fulfilling for all concerned.

It is not our job as practitioners to belittle, challenge or try to change the ethos and views of parents and carers. It is their right to hold those views. It is also our responsibility to provide a supportive and enabling environment for children – both ethically and legally. In order to have a good partnership we need to try our best to work together.

This would also apply when working with parents who have anxieties around men working in the setting because of their cultural and/or their faith background. Again, a vision statement is a useful tool to initiate discussions with the parent and allay their fears. We would always recommend open and respectful discussions about those fears as part of working in partnership with parents in order to secure the best outcomes possible for their children.

Men in childcare

We now move on to the issue of supporting the small number of men who work in childcare. We discuss in a previous book *LGBT Diversity and Inclusion in Early Years Education* (Price and Tayler 2015) the fact that the early years workforce is mainly staffed by women and reasons why this might be.

Case study 6.2

Ben is working in a private day nursery. He is the only male worker. His background is in art and design and he works at the nursery part-time and is an artist specialising in sculpture and installations the rest of the week. When he started at the nursery he had been looking forward to exploring some artistic projects with the children and was especially interested in how he could manage this kind of work with the very youngest children in the nursery.

Since he started at the nursery though he has only worked with the oldest children – the room leader told him 'We have some disruptive boys and thought they would listen to a man'. He has also noticed that he is always on the rota for the outside time and given the group who want to play football. He rarely has time to engage in any creative art activities with the children, inside or outside.

He has also realised that there is an unspoken expectation that he will carry out minor repair tasks such as changing a light bulb or replacing a broken handle. He has made one attempt to ask to be transferred to the baby room. The manager seemed very uncomfortable and said that there were 'issues'. When he questioned her

---

further she said that 'Our parents wouldn't be happy with a man changing a baby's nappies'.

Points to consider

- What are the real issues here?

- Do you see any similarities in Ben's role and the role of any men who are working in any setting that you have had experience of?

Discussion

Something we would like you to think about is how the nursery is replicating traditional gender roles here.

It may be that women are not aware of men doing these practical jobs because the role is 'naturally' one for men, in an environment where caring for children has traditionally been a 'natural' role for women. The ascriptions of 'natural' roles to men and women replicate traditional notions of parenting, and, as in childcare work, are an extension of the conception of childcare as 'women's work'.

(Cameron et al. 1999: 78–79)

Role models

We hope that you can see from the case study and quote above that, as managers, we need to constantly audit our perceptions of what is 'natural' in terms of gender. As well as operating within the legislative framework and responsibilities that we have in early years (see Chapter 3) we are also influenced and guided by our own moral compass. This is a result of the parenting that we had and the role models that we were shown in our formative years. These may not be the same as those of the children and families that we are providing a service for.

In secondary school in the 1960s I (Deborah) was constantly bewildered by the teachers' assumptions that 'mother' was at home and had an endless supply of cooking materials, Tupperware containers and haberdashery. My mother went out to work and, although a gifted and imaginative cook, didn't fit the conventional domestic role that the teachers clearly had in mind and that had been provided by their own backgrounds before World War Two.

Another anecdotal incident – a single mother of one child, a girl, was aware that from an early age her daughter had seen and only had her mother at home carrying out all the jobs that were needed. Some of these were conventionally female as in washing, cooking, cleaning, but some included carpentry, gardening and general domestic DIY. Her daughter started going to pre-school and soon after was pointing to pictures of tools in books and saying 'That's for the daddies', even though she had never seen any man in her house use the tools.

As a manager of a setting, part of our job is to ensure that we are providing good role models for children and that those role models are diverse and don't just reflect the ethos and experiences that the practitioners are comfortable or familiar with. They should also support and enhance the widest experiences possible that will not only include the direct experiences of the children in the setting but also those of the wider world which they may encounter.

Interestingly, some parents may be supportive of men working in the nursery precisely because they wish them to fulfil a traditional 'male' role that may be lacking in their child's life and so may not be so supportive if they see that worker taking part in more 'female' areas of the setting's world.

> Sam hasn't got a father in his life and I have mainly female relatives and friends. I want him to see what a man can be like and have a positive role model to follow.
>
> (Lucy, mother of a three-year-old boy who
> attends full-time nursery)

In this case a manager might be able to have a discussion with the parent that centres on the rich tapestry of the ways that male workers can be involved in the setting's work and the interests and capabilities of all staff.

In the research project that Cameron et al. (1999) carried out, it was interesting that parents could see the benefits of men working with boys, especially if the boys were in a single, female parent family. There was less enthusiasm and relevance seen for men caring for girls. One set of parents was surveyed regarding a man working in their child's nursery where that man was a manager and didn't work with the children directly. They were positive about the male worker but said that if he started to work more closely with children they might revise their views: 'A man dealing with my daughter, I would rather know him more personally' (Cameron et al. 1999: 114).

There are many practical ways in which managers can make sure that they provide a diverse experience for children based on ideas that have occurred in this discussion, including but not limited by:

- ensuring that staff members are rotated around different activities according to interests and capabilities and not gender roles;

- ensuring that children see all staff in active roles – mending, fixing, playing outdoors as much as possible – again allowing for individual interests and needs. It may be that a staff member strongly asserts that this is their choice and it just happens to be stereotypically male or female. In this case we would recommend spending some time as a staff team questioning our assumptions about gender and also emphasising the benefits of being flexible when thinking about the roles and responsibilities we have as staff members in the setting. In the same way that we might rotate staff around the different age ranges and rooms, it is important for staff to challenge themselves and their own personal development by trying a variety of roles. We can't expect children to have this flexibility if they don't see the adults around them role modelling this;

- to complement this – ensuring that children see all staff in a more caring and nurturing role;

- auditing resources (this is covered in more detail in Chapter 7);

- allowing time in staff meetings for staff to talk about their own experiences and ideas about gender and to talk about the way that both men and women can work in the nursery and their expectations of them.

Whether or not the male worker is consciously troubled by sexual stereotypes, he must navigate in a world full of them; and at almost every step he must contradict them. In doing so, he somehow must not feel like an occupational failure or like a pet rabbit 'the (exceptional) male at the childcare centre' (Seifert 1974 cited in Ruxton 1992: 31).

A quote from a male worker in a large work based nursery where he is the only male worker sums this position up: 'Children see thirteen different ways of being female and only one way of being male.' He also said 'Being a male in a setting means that gender is always present and visible'.

The manager of a setting, male or female, must ensure that the male worker(s), especially if there is just one, doesn't constantly have to prove themselves as representative of men generally. If they are a solitary man in an otherwise female team they might feel that they are always 'on show' and that their actions and activities with children are far more closely scrutinised by other staff members and by parents and carers as they are so visible.

Safeguarding children

We want to return to the case study of Ben (case study 6.2) and the comments that the manager made about Ben working in the baby room and nappy changing. We have had experiences of nurseries where parents have complained about men working in baby rooms that have centred on the issue of personal care for children. If a manager is unsure of the ethics of this situation and perhaps influenced by their own negative feelings about this it can be hard for male staff to feel supported in this role. Because of this we want to talk openly about fears and worries that parents, carers and staff members may have in this situation, and how managers can deal with such fears. We feel that this discussion is best placed in this chapter, as ultimately it is the manager's job to recruit to the staff team and also to deal with any issues that are expressed by parents, carers and/or other staff members. It is also the manager's job to establish the overall ethos of the setting and to ensure that all staff members subscribe to that ethos and are supportive of it.

In this discussion we wish to explore the full range of arguments regarding the position of men in childcare and some of those arguments we know are challenging. Our own position is that we fully support the inclusion of men into the early years workforce. We feel that children need to have people caring for them who represent the society that is around them and that includes men. Having men in the workforce also means that the work of caring for children is seen by society as a higher status job that can be carried out by men and women and is not just an extension of the childcare role that can be seen as 'natural' to women and therefore not a skill.

If children see men in a caring role and taking full part in the setting's life then they are freer to explore their own gender and all of its possibilities. Seeing men in a caring role challenges the view that men can only act in one way and women in another. Men working in a setting also provide a positive role model to all parents and carers who come to the setting.

The employment of men in the care of young children is a topic which generates much discussion. On the one hand there are those who argue that the patriarchal organisation of society, sexual inequality and male violence will never be changed whilst men are allowed to opt out of the most human of activities: caring for children. On the other hand, there are those who think that men are so dangerous – physically, but especially sexually – that they should not be allowed to take part in such a crucially sensitive activity as caring for children, especially when the effects of sexual abuse can persist for generations (Owen 1998: 3).

We can't ignore, but examine critically, a view held by some, that men in childcare should be very strictly monitored (in our opinion perhaps leading to even fewer men in childcare) as they pose too much of a threat to children. We note the undisputed fact that, when examining statistics of abusers of children, there are more men than women. Keith Pringle (1995) cited in Cameron et al. (1999) argues that, since men constitute the greatest threat to children then, rather than concentrate on general procedures for safeguarding children, men should be targeted for specific 'preventative work on themselves' (Cameron et al. 1999: 137) and that the behaviour of men workers should be 'adapted or in some cases "restricted"' to help prevent 'men workers from having their actions misinterpreted as being abusive' (Cameron et al. 1999: 137).

Examples of such restrictions that Pringle discusses are: men's use of touch, restricting their work to being with older children, not having male workers with children with severe disabilities or learning difficulties and working with female co-workers rather than on their own.

There are many counter arguments that we could bring to these proposals. In his chapter in the book edited by Owen et al., Andy Bateman (1998) makes some convincing arguments that show the benefits of having men in childcare. These include the assumption that men can protect children and also that they can take responsibility for their whole selves. He also discusses that men who work in daycare will be very highly motivated as there are so many factors that work against men coming into childcare, including social stigma, parents' and staff teams' suspicion, isolation, pay and conditions as examples. If we are able to increase the numbers of men who work in childcare then men working alongside women in caring for young children will become the norm and not particularly sensitive or worrying for carers and parents.

The more men that are in childcare the less that the men who are already working in it currently – the highly motivated individuals that Bateman refers to – will feel that they are always on show and always having to prove that they can be caring and committed individuals.

By proposing these arguments and emphasising the importance of encouraging more men into caring for children we are not denying at all that some men pose a significantly higher risk to children than women generally. What we are saying is that our main ethos is that a setting should be a safe space for children and staff and that any safeguarding practices that protect children and staff members should apply to both men and women.

Research in the USA and the UK has shown that most abuse of children happens within the domestic home. Within childcare services and the home, abuse incidents involve men more than women (Cameron et al. 1999). However, there are cases of abuse that involve women – even though there is sometimes a link between the woman concerned and a man or men, for example the women have been coerced into the abuse by men. A high profile case in the UK in 2009 involved a female member of staff taking inappropriate pictures of children on her phone and making them available to a paedophile ring (Plymouth Safeguarding Children Board 2010).

The link between female abusers and men is in the early stages of research and little has been published. However, taking into account the fact that women have posed a threat to children in daycare then removing men from daycare centres would not remove the risk to children.

Ways that settings can ensure that all children and staff are protected

This chapter will not go into depth detailing safeguarding children procedures that should be adhered to when working with children and ways that staff members can protect themselves against allegations of abuse. In terms of discussing male workers though there are indicators from literature in the US that reduce the likelihood of abuse occurring – these apply to all workers, not just men:

- Unlimited parental access to settings – an 'open door' policy.

- Thorough screening of staff through checks and also through interviews – especially using interview techniques designed to focus on an applicant's moral compass. In *Leading and Supporting Early Years Teams* (Price and Ota 2014) we discuss some of these strategies.

- Attention to the structural layout of settings that respect the privacy of children in toileting activities but also allows staff to see each other, especially when changing nappies (Kelley 1998 in Cameron et al. 1999).

In addition to these practical suggestions we would also add the following in terms of promoting excellent practice within the culture of a setting:

- A manager should ensure that the setting is a safe place for staff in terms of being able to speak openly. One of the findings of the Plymouth serious case review was that staff members felt uncomfortable with the abuser's behaviour but didn't feel able to voice their anxieties or feel that they would be believed, respected and listened to.

- Ensure that children are also cared for in an environment where there is an ethos of respectful practice where adults listen to them and encourage them to value and speak up for themselves.

In this way the adults and the children can listen to each other with respect and by doing this challenge the idea that there are hierarchies of gender based power and also that adults have power over children. If parents are included in this circle of openness then they can feel reassured that their child is being cared for in a supportive and safe environment. In this way the protection of the setting extends from within the childcare setting to the child wherever they are. If we know that most abuse to children happens in the home then this is even more valuable than just making sure that the setting is a safe space for children.

Again, in the writings of Cameron et al. (1999) studies in Norway and childcare provision there have promoted the view that involving more men in caring for children can be part of the solution and not the problem.

The Norwegian nursery school organisation and culture is a preventative measure in itself. [They] are small, with few children, few adults and a large number of staff members; there are open areas and playgrounds; and parents have a say in the daily life of the nursery school. From the outset it seems almost impossible to commit sexual abuse in a nursery school environment.

(Sataoen 1998 cited in Cameron 1999: 137)

Conclusion

Cameron et al. (1999) also cite the writing of Susan Kelley who poses the question – is the risk of having men in childcare worth the benefits? We would argue strongly that it is. In terms of any safeguarding worries then we would say that managers should ensure that safeguarding practices should protect all children and staff members and that these do not need to be enhanced with male workers.

We would also argue that managers and leaders should make use of the skills and experience of the male workers that work in the setting rather than slot them into an idea of what is 'men's work' within a daycare setting.

We would also argue that children benefit from having a diverse workforce in childcare that goes some way to representing the world around them. They also benefit from seeing men and women working together in a supportive way and seeing men in a caring role. All of this challenges the dominant discourse that caring for children is 'women's work' and is part of a woman's natural skill set and so not valued in terms of prestige and status in the workforce.

By supporting men in the workforce we hope that the role of women will also become more diverse. It is important for children to see not only men in a caring role, but women in a more active and less stereotypical role. The ideas and discussions that we have looked at in this chapter should encourage managers and leaders to provide an environment where all staff are working at the peak of their capabilities and interests.

References

Bateman, A. (1998) Child Protection, Risk and Allegations. In C. Owen, C. Cameron and P. Moss (eds) *Men as Workers in Services for Young Children: Issues of a Mixed Gender Workforce,* London: Institute of Education.

Cameron, C., Moss, P. and Owen, C. (1999) *Men in the Nursery*. London: Sage.

Owen, C. (1998) Men as Workers in Services for Young Children: Prolegomena. In C. Owen, C. Cameron and P. Moss (eds) *Men as Workers in Services for*

Young Children: Issues of a Mixed Gender Workforce, London: Institute of Education.

Plymouth Safeguarding Children Board (2010) *Serious Case Review into Abuse at Little Ted's Nursery* [Online]. Available at www.plymouth.gov.uk/homepage/. . ./littletednurseryreview.htm (accessed 15 September 2015).

Price, D. and Ota, C. (2014) *Leading and Supporting Early Years Teams*. Oxon: Routledge.

Price, D. and Tayler, K. (2015) *LGBT Diversity and Inclusion in Early Years Education*. Oxon: Routledge.

Ruxton, S. (1992) *'What's He Doing at the Family Centre?': The Dilemmas of Men who Care for Children*. London: National Children's Homes.

7 | Resources

This chapter will encourage you to consider what is important when thinking about resources in terms of gender. While acknowledging the importance of a good range of high quality resources, you are also asked to think about the centrality of practitioners, parents and children as a resource. Children learn through relationships and by the way in which their interests are supported by those around them.

Part of the commitment practitioners make is to provide an inclusive learning environment and thinking about your own views in relation to gender will be a crucial part of this. These issues will be explored in relation to books, imaginative play, dressing up, the home corner, small world toys and displays. Your thinking is supported by two case studies and other examples from practice.

What are resources?

When asked to think about all the resources they have in their setting, a group of early years practitioners came up with the following list:

- art and craft materials
- malleable materials
- role-play equipment (including home corner and dressing up)
- jigsaw puzzles and other table top toys and games
- large and small construction sets and wooden blocks

- books, posters and displays

- writing area resources

- small world toys

- climbing frame, large wheeled toys and other outdoor equipment

- resources for particular curriculum areas, e.g. maths and literacy

- sand and water trays and equipment for these

- ICT resources

- musical instruments

- cooking equipment.

While all of these resources are of central importance in any early years setting, there are some things missing from this list.

- Practitioners and children. You are the most valuable resource of all in any setting. Children learn through relationships with adults and with their peers. All the equipment in the world cannot (and should not) replace the human interaction that takes place between people. The equipment listed above are the resources that you use to scaffold and support children's development and learning but it is meaningless without relationships.

- Parents. In some settings parents are a crucial part of the running of a setting (for example in a parent-run playgroup). Even when this is not the case, parents are the most important people in a child's life, and will be involved with the setting in varying degrees.

- Activities and experiences. The way you plan the use of the equipment you have is a vitally important part of resourcing. A setting may have a fantastic selection of books for example, but if these are put away in a box for a 'special occasion' they will be of no use to the children.

Taking all these factors into account is nowhere more important than in your commitment to providing good, inclusive provision. If you have a wide range of dressing-up clothes that the children have free access to you have made a start in thinking about your provision. However, if the children choose those clothes along strict gender lines and a child who makes a different choice isn't supported, you are not making use of your most important resource – you and the relationships you have with the children.

Thinking about these issues and working out ways to approach them and to make your use of resources more inclusive is challenging and can be daunting. Wolpert (2005) suggests that you can start this process by thinking about the way we use words and whether we assume they describe masculine or feminine attributes.

Look at the following words. Do you see them as describing boys, girls, neither or both?

- Active
- Gentle
- Brave
- Frightened
- Competitive
- Weak
- Intelligent
- Silly
- Passive
- Strong
- Logical
- Quiet
- Messy
- Conformer
- Emotional
- Rough
- Chatty
- Dependent
- Leader
- Illogical
- Unemotional.

(adapted from Wolpert 2005)

You may have found it easy to attribute some of these words to boys or girls. For example, you may feel that boys tend to be active while girls tend to be passive or that girls are emotional and boys are unemotional. However, for every example of a child who might fit with these stereotypes, you can probably think of an example of a child who doesn't conform to this.

The important thing is to be aware of your own assumptions around these stereotypes and to make sure that your use of resources and the way you interact with the children allows them the opportunities to explore all ways of being so that girls can experience being rough and messy and boys can experience being quiet and gentle.

The role of the adult

As discussed above, the adults in a setting are of central importance in creating the ethos of a setting and the commitment practitioners show to establishing an atmosphere that challenges gender stereotyping is crucial.

Practitioners, as one of the main resources in a setting, can work towards creating this ethos by thinking about the following pointers. This is by no means an exhaustive list and you may think of things you wish to add. This will be a work in progress rather than something that is done once.

- Are you open to thinking about different cultural approaches to an understanding of gender?

- Are you willing to think about your own feelings and beliefs about gender?

- Do you and your team openly discuss your views on gender?

- Do you discuss relevant issues in the press and other media?

- Do you think about how you use language relating to gender?

- Do you confidently respond to sexism or gender stereotypes when expressed by others including children?

- Do you ever use jokes or banter in a sexist way?

- Do you regularly review your resources for stereotypical portrayals of gender?

- Do you observe the children for clues as to their thinking about gender?

- Do you involve parents in your discussions about gender?

- Do you provide a wide range of experiences for children that include, for example, men and women in a range of roles?

- Do you create an environment that supports diversity?

Having thought about the use of language and challenged any assumptions you may have about how these apply to children it can be useful to move on to consider the resources themselves and how these are used and how you relate to the children.

Spend some time observing the use of resources in your setting.

- Who plays with what?

- What areas are used by girls and what areas are used by boys?

- Are some children excluded in some areas?

- Do some children dominate some areas?

- Who takes on what role in the home corner or other imaginative role-play?

- Are some of your resources for imaginative play open ended so that children can use them in creative ways?

- Do you provide positive images of children and adults taking part in a range of activities (posters, displays, books, etc.)?

What about your relationships and interactions with the children?

- Do you avoid language such as asking for 'big strong boys' or 'helpful girls' when tasks need doing?

- Do you support children who cross gender boundaries in their play?

- Do you engage with children in discussions about gender stereotypes?

- Do you join in with imaginative play so that you can challenge gender stereotypes and extend the play in creative ways?

- What approach do you take to war, weapon and superhero play? (See Chapter 5 for further discussion.)

- Do you avoid assumptions about who will want to play with what, or how they will play with it?

- Do you carefully challenge any gender stereotypes expressed by the children or by other adults?

(adapted from Martin 2011)

Case study 7.1

Finn is three years and two months old. He has recently started at a setting that takes children from three years. He attends every morning and a full day on Fridays. He has an older sister who attends the local school. His mother is a single parent although Finn does see his father once a fortnight.

Finn's key person, Jenny, has noticed that Finn particularly enjoys imaginative play, small world toys and looking at books. He often spends lots of time in an assortment of dressing-up clothes and enjoys being in the role-play area. He doesn't join in rougher play or play on the larger equipment in the outdoor area.

Jenny is not concerned about Finn's play preferences and as with all her key children she plans according to Finn's interests. She does try to encourage him to engage in physical activity as she thinks it is important for his physical health but she never pushes this.

One of the other practitioners thinks Finn is unusual for a boy and that he should be encouraged to play with other boys. She thinks his interest in dressing up could be used to encourage him to join in the superhero play that many of the boys his age enjoy. Finn's mother has expressed no anxiety about the way Finn plays.

Points to consider

- What do you think your response would be to the way Finn chooses to play?

- What is your reaction to the perspectives of Finn's key person and of the other practitioner?

- Do you think Jenny should involve Finn's mother in the discussions?

Discussion

This is a good example of how it is the way in which resources are used and the way children are supported that is more important than the resources themselves. If Finn were in a setting that discouraged his play, his experience would be very different than if he were in a setting that supported him, even if the resources were very similar.

It could be useful to start discussion with thinking about why this is considered to be a problem. Why does the practitioner think that Finn needs to be guided towards what she perceives as gender appropriate play? Do we want to operate our early years provision on an assumption that there are boys' activities and girls' activities? If our practice is based on planning in response to the children's interests, don't we have a responsibility to provide that for *all* children?

As all parents should be involved in their children's experiences in early years settings, Finn's mother would hopefully be engaged in ongoing dialogue with Jenny and other practitioners. As she has not expressed any concern about Finn it is safe to assume that the relationship between her and the setting is based on a desire to support Finn in engaging in play that is meaningful for him.

Books

Books are a central resource in most early years settings with children looking at books independently, with peers and with adults. The messages conveyed through text and illustrations can have a powerful impact on how children feel about themselves and others. If all children see are images of children and adults in stereotypical roles, they are less likely to develop awareness that many options are open to them and to others. While these will not be the only influences open to children it is important to consider their impact within your setting.

Older readers of this book, and indeed the two authors, learned to read at a time when characters in children's books were very much drawn along narrowly defined gender roles. Typical storylines showed little girls helping mummy bake a cake while little boys helped daddy wash the car. These storylines also only portrayed white, middle-class, heterosexual families living in nice houses with gardens where everyone is able-bodied, where daddy goes out to work and mummy stays home and wears an apron.

While the richness of children's books today is to be celebrated and enjoyed with children it is important to remember that children are capable of being critical thinkers and challenging the assumptions that some books may convey. Jackson and Gee (2005) in a study of children's reading books remind us that it is important to view the child as 'active in the construction of gender rather than an inkblot soaking up the contents of each page' (117). They remind us that:

There is good evidence to suggest that children bring information from a host of other sources (e.g. television, films, toys, experiences, books) to their reading of gender in a particular resource . . . On the other hand it is also important that publishers, illustrators and writers accept the responsibility for providing children with representations incorporating multiple ways of being male and female.

(Jackson and Gee 2005: 127)

As early years practitioners you are in a good position to support children in their thinking about the gender roles they encounter in books.

Case study 7.2

Kate is a teaching assistant in a reception class. She is very interested in gender and tries to avoid any assumptions about children's interests based on their gender. She recently became interested in thinking about assumptions in children's books and started looking differently at the books in the classroom. Although they have a good range of books that show boys and girls and men and women in a variety of roles she did find that some of the classic books that are generally found in every classroom did convey some stereotypical views of gender. As they could not afford to restock their books, Kate wondered if the existing books could be used as discussion points with the children.

She decided to start with *The Tiger Who Came to Tea* (Kerr 1968). This much-loved classic portrays a little girl at home with her mother when unexpectedly there is a knock on the door. They go to the door and find a tiger there!

The story goes on to explore what happened when they let the tiger in. The tiger proceeded to eat all the food, drink all the water in the tap and even drink all of daddy's beer. The tiger then left and when daddy got home from work they had to go to a café to have some tea.

Kate felt that the image of the mother at home and the father at work may be familiar to some of the children, but certainly not all of them. She knew, for example, that in the class there was a child with a single father at home, several with single mothers, a child in foster care, several children who attended before and after school club and had two working parents and several more for whom no one worked through unemployment or ill health. She also felt that the story conveyed some very strong underlying stereotypes. The world of Sophie and her mother is very domestic and they only venture out when the father returns and the beer is definitely daddy's.

Kate read the story with a small group of children and asked them what they thought about it. Initially they said how much they liked the story and how they wished a tiger would come to their house. Kate asked them if they think Sophie's mum goes out to work too and if her dad sometimes stays home. This led to a discussion about who works in their families and who stays home. One child said that if a tiger came to his house he would be scared and would hide. Kate asked if Sophie seemed scared of the tiger and they all agreed that she wasn't scared and even cuddled the tiger! One of the girls declared that Sophie was very brave and added that if a tiger came to her house she would be brave too and cuddle it like Sophie did.

Points to consider

- Do you have some books in your setting that you think convey a stereotyped view of gender?

- Have you tried discussing this with the children? If not, is this something you could do?

- Do you think there is still a place for classics stories like this or do you think all the books in your setting should provide a more egalitarian view?

Discussion

Kate felt that there were problems with the storyline in *The Tiger Who Came to Tea* but instead of believing the children shouldn't have access to it, she used it as an opportunity to discuss the issues with the children. She particularly felt the domestic scene conveyed a life style that didn't relate to the experiences of many of the children in her setting.

However, what surprised her was that the children noticed something she had missed. It was a boy who said he would be frightened and this led them to acknowledging that Sophie had been very brave. This countered many images of boys as brave and girls as in need of protection and gave her a new way of thinking about this book. It also made her reevaluate her assumption that she was best placed to decide what books were most appropriate for children in terms of gender stereotypes.

What to look out for in books

While acknowledging that children bring their own understanding and ways of challenging what they see in books, there are things you as a practitioner can look out for.

- Do the illustrations and/or storyline convey stereotypes of how girls and boys and women and men look, think, act or behave? Are boys active and girls passive? Are men engaged in paid work and women in domestic work?

- Even when someone is shown outside these stereotypical roles, are they just a one-off token or are a variety of roles shown throughout the book?

- Do storylines involving girls and women show them achieving on their own merit or do storylines often evolve how they look, e.g. being a beautiful princess?

- What impact might the storyline or illustrations have on the self-image of girls and boys? Will all children see a variety of characters that they could identify with?

- Check the language used in the book. Books that could be gender neutral (e.g. about teddy bears) often use 'he' as a generic term.

- Are girls described in a more passive way while boys are depicted as brave?

- Do you have books that specifically try to provide positive images in terms of gender?

Imaginative play, dressing up and the home corner

Children engage in imaginative play from a very young age and this becomes more complex as children get older. By the time children finish the early years foundation stage they will probably be engaging in complex imaginative games that endure over time and may be revisited on several occasions. The role of the practitioner is to support this play with sensitivity and with a view to engaging with the children in a way likely to extend the play rather than control it.

This area of play is often one of the most contentious in terms of gender and can evoke some strong feelings from practitioners and parents. Superhero play was discussed in detail in Chapter 5 and this is one area where imaginative play is often allowed to flourish for boys. This in itself can be seen as problematic when other aspects of imaginative play aren't engaged in by boys. It conveys a message that boys are powerful, strong and engaging in exciting scenarios outside everyday life. If the imaginative play of girls is predominantly domestic in nature this can lead to a split in how girls and boys are viewed by practitioners and by each other.

The ideal is for all forms of imaginative play to be open to all children. When children are putting on dressing-up clothes, they are literally putting on an experience. They are seeing how it feels to wear this, to be this character, to be someone different. While 'children, both boys and girls, like to dress up because they are trying out how to be adults, as well as creating characters in their play' (Lindon 2012) they are also experiencing how other children may feel. Experiencing how others may feel is crucial in the development of empathy so dressing up is a very important part of a child's social and emotional development.

Viewing a diversity of ways of dressing up through this lens can be more helpful than worrying about boys wearing a princess dress or girls dressing as Batman. Children like to try things out and this often has little to do with the future. Sometimes concern about boys and girls dressing up in ways that challenge gender norms is met with the reassurance that a little boy trying on a princess dress does not mean he will be gay. We would suggest that the fact that this issue is approached as one that needs reassurance is not in keeping with an ethos of inclusion for all. It is important to remember that all the little boy in the princess dress is doing at the moment

> is exploring what it might be like to wear the clothes he has seem some adults wear. He might also be drawn to the particular colours and textures of the item he has chosen. They may be sparkly and glittery and catch his eye. He will have seen his other friends try them on and wants to share their experience.
>
> (Price and Tayler 2015: 111)

Home corners are very common features of early years settings and are the site of much imaginative role-play. One early years practitioner talked to us about how she resources their home corner.

> I have worked in several settings before coming here and in all of them the home corner was where a limited selection of activities related to living in a home took place. Usually there are things related to kitchens like cookers, cupboards, pots and pans and plates, etc. Then there are usually things related to caring for babies like dolls, cots and bedding. In the setting where I work now, we take the view that all sorts of things take place in homes and that needs to be reflected in the resources we have. We have all the usual things but we also have a computer, books, pens and paper, tools, paintbrushes, clothes, plants and ornaments. The children are encouraged to take resources from other areas of the setting and use them in the home corner. Since expanding the way we resource the home corner, we have found there is a much more balanced number of boys and girls using it.

Have a look at the resources in your home corner.

- What range of resources do you have?
- What roles within the home do they reflect?
- What could you add to make this more diverse?

- Do you have a balance of boys and girls accessing your home corner?

- If not, what could you do to address this?

- Could you also have an outdoor home corner? What impact might this have on how boys and girls access it?

Many settings have role-play areas in addition to the home corner. These can reflect children's interests and build on topics being explored in other areas of provision. They are all ideal opportunities to encourage boys and girls to engage in creative and imaginative play. They may include:

- Hospitals and clinics

- Garages and petrol stations

- Hairdressers

- Shops

- Travel agents

- Offices

- Post offices

- Railway station.

Case study 7.3

Amira is a childminder who has cared for children in her own home for 14 years. Before that she worked in a nursery for eight years so she is very experienced and has a Foundation Degree in early years which she hopes to top up to a full degree in the next couple of years. She cares for three children under five although one is now in reception part-time and she fetches him at lunch time. She has the unusual experience that for the last four years she has only cared for boys. Whenever she has had a space in that time it has been filled by another boy. She is committed to equality and doesn't feel it makes any difference to how she should resource her setting. She has a well-equipped role-play area and lots of dressing-up clothes as well as bikes, bricks and a good range of other toys and equipment. Her experience is that all the boys she has cared for access the full range of equipment and enjoy the range of experiences she has on offer. She has had some comments from parents such as 'Well, you don't really need dolls here do you?' and even 'How's he going to get a girlfriend if you keep only having boys?' Although said in jest, these comments concern her and sometimes she is unsure how to respond.

Points to consider

- Do you think having only boys or only girls in your setting would make a difference to your provision of resources? If so, why?

- Do you think there are any implications of being in a single sex group for the children?

- How do you think Amira could respond to the comments made by some parents?

Discussion

Although unusual, Amira's situation is not unique. Many private schools are single sex and have nursery provision. You may feel that it is a disadvantage for children not to experience being in a mixed group and that there is much that girls and boys can learn from each other. While it might not make a difference in terms of resources provided, Amira might consider taking the children to drop-in sessions somewhere where they will mix in a more diverse group. The oldest child is now at school so he will be experiencing this in his new environment.

Talking to parents openly and honestly is a central part of any relationships with parents, whatever the setting. Having a clear policy about equality and inclusion will help support Amira with this.

Small world toys

When young children play in a role-play area or with dressing-up clothes they are trying out being one character. They may be a doctor, Spiderman, a fairy, a fire-fighter, a dog or a character from a favourite story. They may change character quickly or keep the same one over a period of time. They can only ever be one character at a time though.

The difference with small world play is that the child can be many characters and can control all their actions and behaviour. With a small world hospital for example, the child can be doctor, nurse and patient as they play out a scenario. This gives the child a sense of power in how a story plays out and provides opportunities for the child to interact with peers and adults to build a story.

Many small world toys involve people and it is important to make sure that the play people provided represent girls and boys and women and men in a variety of roles and that the language you use when you are supporting play reflects diversity.

- Use fire-fighter instead of fireman and police officer instead of policeman, etc.

- Don't assume nurses are female and doctors are male.

- Avoid setting small world toys out so that garages, for example, are only populated by men.

- Provide enough people to give children options in how they play with them.

Many other small world toys consist of sets of animals whether farm animals, zoo animals, wildlife, sea creatures or dinosaurs. While it might seem gender is not an issue here it is vitally important that the use of the term 'he' is not used in a generic way. Try to use 'she' just as often. For example, 'Wow! That T-Rex is big! I wonder where she lives'.

There are many providers of a good range of small world toys (The Consortium Education 2015, Early Years Resources 2015, Hope Education 2015, TTS 2015) and the important point, especially with play people, is to choose sufficient for children to use them flexibly.

Displays

When children and families first enter a setting it is often the displays that will first catch their eye. What do your displays say about your setting?

- Do they show that everyone is welcome?

- Do they convey messages of equality and diversity?

- Do they show all sorts of people engaged in all sorts of roles and activities?

- Can children see themselves and their families reflected around them?

- Do they challenge stereotypical views of who can do what?

Tracey is a teaching assistant in a reception class. They were doing a topic on 'People who help us' and they had a range of resources to support this. They had a series of jigsaw puzzles on display that the children had free access to. One showed a male police office, another had five male fire-fighters and another had a postman. Tracey didn't feel happy with this representation or the messages it gave the children about what roles were open to them.

She and the class teacher decided the best way forward was for the children to make their own displays. They also felt this would allow opportunities for discussion about the roles of the men and women who help us. They used circle time to discuss who helps us. Many children had experiences with doctors and nurses and some children had had contact with the police or fire-fighters. Further discussion and role-play were used to explore who carries out these roles. This led to painting, drawing, collage and junk modelling to convey the roles they had discussed. The displays they created were much more lively and diverse than commercially provided resources and they carried more meaning for the children as they had created them themselves.

Conclusion

This chapter has asked you to consider resources in a wider sense than simply the physical resources that exist in your setting. You have been asked to think about relationships between children and their peers and between children and the adults around them. The resources in your setting are part and parcel of these relationships and the way they are used to support children's interests will have a profound impact on their understanding of gender.

You have also been asked to think about the power and agency that children have themselves in relation to their understanding of gender. Children don't simply absorb understandings from adults; they are co-creators of that understanding as is shown clearly in the example of the practitioner who used traditional stories to discuss gender with the children at her setting.

Alongside this understanding that children are not passive recipients of culture, it is important to think about the resources you provide, the language you use when discussing resources with children and the opportunities you create to enable children to explore in a rich and varied environment.

References

The Consortium Education (2015) *Small World* [Online]. Available at www.educationsupplies.co.uk/early-years/small-world (accessed 15 September 2015).

Early Years Resources (2015) *Early Years Resources: Wooden and Plastic Figures* [Online]. Available at www.earlyyearsresources.co.uk/search/small-world (accessed 15 September 2015).

Hope Education (2015) *Hope Education: Small World Play* [Online]. Available at www.hope-education.co.uk/products/early-years/small-world (accessed 15 September 2015).

Jackson, S. and Gee, S. (2005) 'Look Janet', 'No You Look John': Constructions of Gender in Early School Reader Illustrations Across 50 Years. *Gender and Education*, 17(2): 115–128.

Kerr, J. (1968) *The Tiger Who Came to Tea*. London: HarperCollins.

Lindon, J. (2012) *Equality and Inclusion in Early Childhood*. London: Hodder Education.

Martin, B. (2011) *Children at Play: Learning Gender in the Early Years*. London: Trentham.

Price, D. and Tayler, K. (2015) *LGBT Diversity and Inclusion in Early Years Education*. London: Routledge.

TTS (2015) *TTS: Small World* [Online]. Available at www.tts-group.co.uk/shops/tts/Catalogue/Small-World/9d50de6b-5b54-4951-8470-dec893b06926 (accessed 15 September 2015).

Wolpert, E. (2005) *Start Seeing Diversity*. Boston: Redleaf Press.

8 | Conclusion

We hope that you have enjoyed reading this book and that it has challenged and informed your practice. Our intention in writing this book is that practitioners will read sections of it that they find interesting and appropriate and by doing this gradually read it rather than read through from start to finish. We also hope that this book remains in the staff room for practitioners to continue to consult for ideas on resources, further reading and having difficult conversations with and supporting the children and families that they work with.

We anticipate that any training which staff teams engage in as a result of this book that focuses on gender will also feed into their work in equalities generally. In this book we are specifically looking at gender but we are also committed to settings supporting families in all of their diverse forms – single parents, two mothers, two fathers, grandparents as carers, foster carers, adoptive parents and many other variations on this. We note in our book *LGBT Diversity and Inclusion in Early Years Education* (2015) that 'Children and families come in all shapes and sizes' (Price and Tayler 2015, front page) and gender is just part of a much bigger picture of diversity that settings should be celebrating and engaging with.

Our aim is for settings not just to keep up with current legal requirements and EYFS standards but also to be at the forefront of outstanding practice in terms of diversity. We believe achieving this level of practice is not just about doing what is needed to meet standards but reflectively thinking about what can be done in order to lead the setting onto the next step in equalities work with children and with staff teams.

In this conclusion we want to finish by looking at some key ideas and also some ways forward in order for settings to be able to use practical ideas that they can put in place to audit and commit to excellent practice in gender diversity in their settings. We want each reader's development not to just end here, with the reading of this book, but to continue and develop into the future. We also want the book to influence the practice of settings and in order to facilitate this we have listed some next steps below. These can form a timetable of change and refining in gender practice. In this way we hope that this book can become a working resource which is not gathering dust on a shelf in the staff room, but is regularly consulted and used as inspiration, for information and also to inform and guide further discussion.

Voices of children

Activity

We asked some pre-school children what they thought about being a boy or a girl:

> Sometimes I like to wear the princess dress at school and the other boys are mean to me.
>
> (boy aged 3)

> I don't like to get my hands dirty with mud but paint's OK.
>
> (girl aged 4)

> Being a girl is lovely because you can wear pink.
>
> (girl aged 3)

> Boys are better than girls because girls are silly and cry all the time.
>
> (boy aged 4)

What would you say to these children if they were speaking to you? This would be a good starting point for staff discussion. It is a sensitive and tricky task to respond appropriately to the last two statements in a way that affirms the child's right to have opinions and yet also challenges the stereotypical views about boys and girls that they are expressing. We would suggest the following types of responses:

I think that boys can wear pink as well? I saw Miriam's dad the other day wearing a pink shirt and he looked great, did you see him?

Sometimes when I get up I want to wear pink and sometimes I want to wear green. Do you have days like that?

I think that when people get upset they feel like crying and they can be a boy or a girl – what do you think?

I think that boys and girls are fab – especially all the ones who come to this nursery. Let's think of the names of all the children that you're friends with and say them together.

Activity

For these next quotes we asked children what they liked doing at pre-school and we haven't put the gender of the child in these ones. We suggest that you try to guess them and then question your assumptions – why did you think that? What did you think when you found out the answer? For your information we've put the answers just above the next activity.

When I get scared I like to cuddle my blanket.

(child aged 3)

I like it when I can ride the pink bike with the bell.

(child aged 2)

In the home corner I make cakes and put the little things on top.

(child aged 4)

My best thing is to be outside and to climb the slide thing.

(child aged 2)

Key themes of the book

(These refer to Chapter 2.)

- Gender is socially constructed.

- Biology alone does not explain the range of different ways that there are to be a man or a woman.

- The physical differences between girls and boys do not explain away the different ways that they are treated.

These are the main ideas that we want you to reflect on as a result of this book. From reading the book we hope that you can see the elements of good practice that we think need to be in place in order for a setting to know that it is providing a thoughtful and supportive environment for children, staff and parents/carers in terms of gender. We have summarised and listed these below.

Key features of an outstanding setting that has an inclusive ethos

- Children have freedom to self select activities and resources and explore gender generally.

- There is an enabling, supportive and open environment with resources that are regularly audited to ensure that they reflect the diversity of gender roles that are in society as well as other aspects of diversity.

- There is respectful engagement with staff, children and parents and carers.

- The staff team includes men and women and ensures that staff work across the breadth of activities, age ranges and tasks in the setting. Both men and women are in management roles.

- There is regular staff time for whole staff discussion and reflection on gender and sharing of the team's own ethos and areas that they find challenging.

Answers to the activity are: boy, boy, girl, girl.

Activity: a menu for change

This is a clear way of thinking about a programme for change that can be enabled in bite sized (!) portions and can be used as a template for a setting and its ways forward in terms of gender diversity for a term.

Appetiser

Think of a small change that you can make in your setting tomorrow. This could be putting up a poster that celebrates the different ways that men and women can be themselves, ordering some books that celebrate diversity, putting 'gender' on the staff meeting agenda or changing the wording in a song you sing to make it less stereotypical.

Another idea is to use a Persona Doll (www.persona-doll-training. org) to 'talk' to the children and explore ideas about gender. Perhaps the doll has been stopped playing football or making necklaces because they are a boy or a girl? Children have a strong sense of what is fair and unfair and usually enjoy discussing this type of situation.

Set up a messy, muddy, splashy activity and encourage all children to join in.

Starter

Something you could do next week.

Thinking about language and communication as a weeklong focus for the staff team – they should meet at the beginning to talk through the project and discuss how they are going to implement it. They should also meet at the end of the week and review how it has progressed and how the project has worked – what went well and what was difficult?

Think about how you speak to children. Often people compliment girls on what they look like and boys on what they are doing, or tell boys not to cry, and girls to 'smile' and be 'nice'. Research indicates that adults are more likely to engage in conversation with girls than boys. They may even use a different tone of voice. It's good to speak to all children in the same way and about the same things. You could practise the following:

1. Tell a girl she's great because of what she does and not because of how she looks; try, 'I like your skipping' not 'I like your hair'.
2. Praise a boy when he shares and displays co-operative behaviour with other children.
3. Tell a girl it's OK to say if there's something she's good at.
4. Encourage girls to play in the mud or get sweaty.
5. Encourage boys to play in the home corner, or with dolls.
6. Tell girls it's OK to get angry and to express this in a healthy way.
7. Tell boys it's OK to be scared, upset or emotional.
8. Tell a boy that it's OK to dress up as a nurse or butterfly and a girl that it's OK to dress up as a fire-fighter or pirate.
9. Tell a boy that being called a girl isn't an insult, because boys and girls are equally important.
10. Encourage all children to think about things that they have in common with each other, and emphasise their similarities over differences.

(Zero Tolerance 2013: 15)

As a team you might decide to all carry notebooks with you in order to make quick reflective jottings about the language you have used and if you have made a conscious effort to engage with any of the points above. A project like this is a sensitive one that challenges beliefs that individuals may have absorbed and held from their own childhood. Such a programme would have to be a whole staff initiative and would have to be managed skilfully. We would suggest that it would have to be carried out in a setting that has worked to achieve an ethos in the staff team where members can hold each other accountable and speak freely and honestly with each other about their achievements and also places where they struggle. This would not be an activity to carry out in a newly formed team or one where there were tensions and staff found it hard to interact respectfully or truthfully with each other.

Main course

This is at least a month-long ongoing project. We would suggest the following actions as possibilities:

- As a staff team rewrite (or write) the setting's vision statement – see our suggestions in Chapter 6 for this.

- Set up a series of staff meetings or in-house training where the team look at their own ideas about gender and think of ways to make the setting a more inclusive place in terms of the way that they speak to each other, the children and the parents, the way that the nursery is organised in terms of staff rotas, layout and colours it is painted.

- Audit and review the resources that are available to children: books, toys, puzzles, dressing-up clothes, home corner equipment, outside equipment. Are there some that could be discarded and are there ways that others could be updated or changed? Review the budget – could you order some books and puzzles that show a more balanced view of the world?

- Audit and review the activities that you offer to children – are they varied in terms of children's preferences or have you unconsciously thought of gender when setting them ('We need to have something for the boys')?

- Do the same when thinking about the space you use. For example are all of the outdoor activities active? Is there a place where more artistic and creative projects could take place outside? Could you put everything away inside and have a huge throwing session with pillows?

* We talk in Chapter 6 about staff rotas and making assumptions about gender. In this month you could take time to look at this critically and perhaps discuss it in a staff meeting. You could examine what people's interests are and where they think they could progress or be challenged by trying something new.

Dessert

This should be something fun!

We suggest that staff could play with gender and wear something unusual at work one day – a tool belt, glittery nail varnish, sparkly clothes, dungarees, a hard hat – anything that might get children talking about what men wear and what women wear.

In a staff meeting carry out the assumptions activity that we detail in Chapter 4.

Plan a staff day out where you do something that is a challenge – a Forest school day, flying birds of prey, row boating – anything you agree would stretch you as a team.

We would suggest that when carrying out activities like the ones we detail above, it is also important to build into those activities time for review. Reflective practice entails not only carrying out tasks but also looking at the result of those tasks – how did we feel about them? Did they remind us of anything else? Would we adapt them or change them in any way if we did them again? Without this element of reflective practice they just stand alone as one-off activities and the full value of them is not fully realised.

We also consider that in order to undertake these kind of activities the staff team need to have an ongoing programme of discussion and reflection that feeds into the ethos of the setting. A staff team who barely know each other and have little trust cannot undertake these kinds of projects. They need to be part of the work that a robust team undertakes. Such a team has members who can hold each other accountable, speak freely and are able to give critical and reflective feedback to each other. We want the setting to provide a space where children can freely express themselves and feel able to be who they are and explore possibilities. In the same way we hope that staff will feel a similar freedom and safety.

Finally

Gender work is challenging. Thinking about gender can demand that we examine ideas and assumptions that we have – perhaps unconsciously – assimilated in our early childhood from the adults around us. If we accept one of our key points in this book, that our ideas about gender are socially and culturally constructed, then it follows that we need to unpick and audit these ideas in order to get to the kernel of reality that lies within them.

This can be an uneasy process as we are only too aware. It can be especially difficult for the leaders and managers of settings as they have extra responsibility in terms of children, staff teams and legislative demands. Chapter 6 looks at the sensitive issue of men in childcare and we make no apologies for voicing difficult opinions and ideas about the role of men in childcare. We felt that to gloss over these would be to do the practitioner a disservice and that it was valuable to unpick fears and assumptions and look at ways to move forward positively rather than to pretend that they don't exist. Our position is clear: we support men in childcare and feel that all staff, children, parents and carers should thrive in a setting that has a safe and enabling environment where men and women can be positive role models to children in terms of gender roles. Staff should feel able to work in a way that gives them a space where they can freely work to their strengths and discover new skills and roles. Children can then be supported by staff to explore their own gender roles in a supportive surrounding where they are valued and respectfully engaged with.

One of our aims in this book is to speak to the practitioner who has always questioned gender in early years but hasn't had a framework to think about how those questions may be answered and also how to move their own thinking and the practice of their setting forward. The discussions about gender and the practical activities and thoughts should help to give that practitioner the confidence and information that they need in order to do this. We intend for the ideas, activities, arguments and theory that we talk through to form a package of support.

The ideas that we present in this book can change practice and we hope that they do.

References

Price, D. and Tayler, K. (2015) *LGBT Diversity and Inclusion in Early Years Education*. London: Routledge.

Zero Tolerance (2013) *Just Like a Child: Challenging Gender Stereotyping in the Early Years, a Guide for Professionals* [Online]. Available at www.dayprogramme.org/Challenging%20gender%20stereotyping.pdf (accessed 28 September 2015).

Appendix 1
Children's books

There are many books available for young children that challenge traditional gender roles. Many of these are readily available from good book shops or online. It is important not to see these as specialist books that are brought out in order to highlight the issue. They should be readily available for all children all the time. It is also worth remembering that many traditional tales that might conform to a stereotyped view of gender can be used in discussion with children to challenge these roles. Chapter 7, case study 7.2 has an example of how this can be approached.

Below are some links to lists of books on the theme of challenging gender roles and expectations. This is followed by a selection of picture books for the early years age group.

Letterbox Library (2015) *Gender Equality* [Online]. Available at www.letterboxlibrary.com/acatalog/GENDER_EQUALITY.html (accessed 23 September 2015).

What Do We Do All Day? (2014) *14 Children's Books that Challenge Gender Stereotypes* [Online]. Available at www.whatdowedoallday.com/2014/06/childrens-books-that-challenge-gender-stereotypes.html (accessed 23 September 2015).

Institute for Humane Education (2012) *12 Children's Picture Books that Challenge Traditional Gender Roles* [Online]. Available at http://humaneeducation.org/blog/2012/06/11/12-childrens-picture-books-that-challenge-traditional-gender-roles/ (accessed 23 September 2015).

Good Reads (2015) *Children's Books that Break Gender Stereotypes* [Online]. Available at www.goodreads.com/list/show/34011.Children_s_Books_that_ Break_Gender_Stereotypes (accessed 23 September 2015).

NUT (2014) *It's Child's Play: Challenging Gender Stereotypes Through Reading* [Online]. Available at www.teachers.org.uk/files/childs-play-20pp-final-for-website.pdf (accessed 23 September 2015).

Beaty, A. (2013) *Rosie Revere, Engineer.* New York: Abrams Books for Young Readers.
A wonderful story about a girl who dreams of becoming an engineer. Supported by her Great, Great Aunt, she invents and builds and learns that failure is all part of the process.

Birkett, G. (2009) *Fix it!* Swindon: Child's Play (International).
Includes both boys and girls joining in with DIY projects.

Brubaker Bradley, K. (2006) *Ballerino Nate.* London: Dial Books.
Nate loves ballet. Although he gets teased, he also gets support, particularly when he meets a professional male ballet dancer.

Bunnell, J. (2010) *Sometimes the Spoon Runs Away with Another Spoon: Colouring Book.* Oakland, CA: PM Press.
This is basically a colouring book which celebrates sensitive boys, tough girls and others who might not fit into disempowering gender categories. It is perfect for exploring and celebrating gender variety.

Cole, B. (1996) *Princess Smartypants.* London: Puffin Books.
Princess Smartypants does not want to get married. This hilarious fairytale with a difference tells the story of how she fought for her independence.

Crisp, D. (2006) *Little Drivers Going Places.* Swindon: Child's Play (International).
This book comes with a cutout double-sided figure so that either a boy or a girl can be slipped into the driving seat of these public transport vehicles.

Crisp, D. (2006) *Little Drivers Working Hard.* Swindon: Child's Play (International).
As with *Going Places* the figure in this book can be the driver of a range of working vehicles.

Dobbins, J. (2013) *A Farmer's Life for Me.* Oxford: Barefoot Books.
Shows a group of girls and boys and men and women working together on a farm. Includes girls and women farming and a man baking. Also has a CD to watch and sing along to.

Elliot, M. (2014) *Pearl Power*. Hastings: I Love Mel Publishing.
Pearl Power is a feisty five-year-old who believes very strongly in girl and boy equality. Her first adventure sees her moving house and changing school whilst remaining clever, strong and kind. Upon meeting one boy who seems to think that boys are better than girls, she teaches him a lesson in girl power, as well as in kindness.

Ewart, M. (2008) *10,000 Dresses*. New York: Seven Stories Press.
Bailey dreams of nothing but wearing dresses. He is told he can't wear dresses because 'You're a boy!' but then he meets someone who finds him inspiring and things start to change.

Gray, K. (2009) *Super Daisy*. London: Red Fox.
Super Daisy is a lively character whose mission is to save the world from little green peas!

Gruska, D. (2008) *The Only Boy in Ballet Class*. Layton, UT: Gibbs Smith.
Tucker loves ballet but people don't understand his passion. One day he gets the perfect opportunity to prove what ballet can achieve!

Heep, S. (2004) *Red Rockets and Rainbow Jelly*. London: Puffin Books.
Although primarily about colours this book provides lots of opportunities to discuss similarities and differences and that girls and boys don't always like what they are expected to!

Hoffman, S. and Hoffman, I. (2014) *Jacob's New Dress*. Illinois: Alan Whitman and Company.
Jacob gets teased for wearing a dress to school but gets support from his teacher and his mother. This is a story about self-acceptance and being proud of who you are.

Kemp, A. (2010) *Dogs Don't Do Ballet*. London: Simon & Schuster Children's Publishing.
Biff is not like other dogs. He doesn't chase sticks, he doesn't scratch and he doesn't pee on lamp posts! Biff doesn't know he is a dog. He thinks he is a ballerina.

Kemp, A. (2012) *The Worst Princess*. London: Simon & Schuster Children's Publishing.
Princess Sue likes adventures. They are so much more fun than pretty dresses!

Kilodavis, C. (2011) *My Princess Boy*. London: Simon & Schuster Children's Publishing.
Dyson loves pink, dresses and his tiara. He also likes to climb trees. He's a Princess Boy, and his family loves him exactly as he is.

Kubler, A. (1999) *Man's Work!* Swindon: Child's Play (International).
A little boy and his dad have a fun day tidying and cleaning together.

Munsch, R. (2009) *The Paperbag Princess.* Toronto: Annick Press.
First published in 1980 this is a firm favourite with those who want to challenge
    traditional roles. Princess Elizabeth is brave and resourceful. She sets out to
    rescue her prince from a dragon but the story doesn't end in a traditional
    way!

Newman, L. (2004) *A Fire Engine for Ruthie.* New York: Clarion Books.
Ruthie is staying with her grandmother who has planned playing with dolls
    and having tea parties. Ruthie has other ideas and her grandmother quickly
    joins in.

O'Connor, G. (2010) *If I Had a Velociraptor.* London: Walker Books.
A delightful story about a little girl who imagines what life would be like if she
    had a Velociraptor. The book is unusual in that many dinosaur stories are
    aimed at boys.

Owen, K. (2012) *I Could Be, You Could Be.* Oxford: Barefoot Books.
A boy and a girl imagine themselves as space travelling astronauts. Provides
    inspiration for make-believe play and dressing up. Their imagined worlds
    are beautifully portrayed.

Pomranz, C. (2015) *Made by Raffi.* London: Frances Lincoln Children's Books.
A delightful story about a quiet boy who loves to knit. When he makes a cape
    for school pageant, he saves the day!

Roger, M. and Sol, A. (2013) *What Are You Playing At?* Slough: Alana Books.
The pictures of this book challenge the idea that boys can't play with dolls and
    girls can't play football. It shows that all sorts of people can do all sorts of
    things!

Sharratt, N. and Goodhart, P. (2013) *Just Imagine.* London: Random House.
Rich and colourful illustrations allow plenty of interaction with the reader.
    Would you like to be big or would you like to be small? Lots of opportunities
    to discuss gender and the possibilities that exist.

Sharratt, N. and Goodhart, P. (2004) *You Choose.* London: Random House.
As above with questions like 'What would you wear?' Children could choose
    a superhero outfit, a princess dress, a pair of pyjamas or maybe nothing at
    all!

Teckentrup, B. (2013) *Fast and Slow.* Oxford: Barefoot Books.
This book shows a multicultural and gender positive portrayal of all sorts of
    drivers driving all sorts of vehicles!

Yokococo (2012) *Hans and Matilda*. Dorking, Surrey: Templar.
Matilda and Hans are both little cats but they are SO different! Matilda is such a good girl but Hans is very naughty . . . Are they actually the same cat?

Yolen, J. and Stemple, H. (2010) *Not All Princesses Dress in Pink*. London: Simon & Schuster Children's Publishing.
Princesses using power tools and breaking their nails while still wearing sparkly crowns! Hilarious rhyming text and colourful illustrations.

Appendix 2

Useful websites and organisations

www.letterboxlibrary.com @letterboxlib
Letterbox Library is a 31-year-old, not for profit, children's bookseller specialising in books which celebrate inclusion, equality and diversity. They are famous for their book selection process and all of the books they stock have been approved by an independent team of reviewers that includes early years and primary teachers, librarians, social workers and children. You can see all of their books on their website and you can search under relevant themes, including 'gender'.

www.kathybrodie.com/men-in-childcare-podcast/ @kathybrodie
Kathy Brodie.com has some interesting podcasts about men working in childcare. They cover issues such as men trying to gain equal recognition to women in early years settings, overcoming parents' feelings about men in childcare and how one practitioner is trying to encourage boys to do placements in early years settings.

www.lettoysbetoys.org.uk/why-it-matters/ @lettoysbetoys
Let Toys be Toys is a pressure group that has a blog and other information to persuade manufacturers to stop gendering children's toys. As a result of their campaign, many stores have stopped labelling their toys as 'boys' toys' and 'girls' toys'. This includes Boots, Debenhams, Marks and Spencer and Sainsbury's.

www.nurseryworld.co.uk @NurseryWorld
Nursery World is a fortnightly magazine for all involved in the early years. It includes many useful articles on gender.

www.early-education.org.uk
The British Association for Early Childhood Education. Provides information, courses and publications on a range of issues in the early years, including gender.

https:///ecpuk.org
The Early Childhood Project is a unique and innovative educational charity set up in 1988. They support individuals on the journey around equalities and inclusion. They help develop knowledge and skills that enable them to challenge and combat prejudice, discrimination and injustice in the lives of young children.

http://tactyc.org.uk/news/
TACTYC is a professional organisation for all involved in early years with the aim of enhancing the well-being of all young children. They have equality and diversity as one of their core values.

www.psotc.com/transgender.pdf
This is an interesting collection of articles about transgender children, one that we cite in Chapter 4 (Knight 2014) and others that are good for further reading.

www.teachers.org.uk/educationandequalities/breakingthemould
Breaking the Mould is a project run by the National Union of Teachers (NUT). The website has links to useful resources and articles about their research.

www.pinkstinks.org.uk
Pinkstinks is a campaign that targets the products, media and marketing that prescribe heavily stereotyped and limiting roles to young girls. They believe that all children – girls and boys – are affected by the 'pinkification' of girlhood. Their aim is to challenge and reverse this growing trend.

www.amightygirl.com
A Mighty Girl is a large collection of online books, toys, movies and clothing that encourages confident and courageous girls.

www.bernardvanleer.org/English/Home.html
The Bernard van Leer Foundation aims to improve opportunities for young children in social or economic difficulty with a view to creating equal opportunities and rights for all.

Additional Twitter links

@kathtayler and @debredprice (authors of this book)

@csie_uk
CSIE is a charity working to promote equality and eliminate discrimination in education: wide range of resources, training and consultancy.

@WException
Without Exception – Freelance Editor and Inclusion Consultant. Inclusive Minds – Co-founder.

@InclusiveMinds
Helping ensure books include all children.

Further reading

Ball, R. (2015) *The Gender Police: A Diary* [e-book]. Available at https://itunes.apple.com/gb/book/the-gender-police-a-diary/id1017024648?mt=11 (accessed 5 October 2015).
The Gender Police: A Diary is an intriguing and insightful record of how people treat girls and boys differently. When Ros Ball and James Millar's son was born in 2010 they instantly felt people treated him differently to his big sister. Inspired by the 1980s best-selling diary *There's a Good Girl* and driven by 21st century technology, they started to tweet about the differences they experienced. What began as an attempt to retain their sanity in a gender obsessed world became a life-changing experiment about gender identity.

Blaise, M. (2009) 'What a girl wants, what a girl needs': responding to sex, gender, and sexuality in the early childhood classroom. *Journal of Research in Childhood Education*, 23(3): 450–460.

Taking a poststructuralist view, this article examines the view that children are active in developing their understandings of gender. It will be of interest to anyone who wishes to explore the content of Chapter 2 further.

Braw, E. (2014) The three letter word driving a gender revolution. *Newsweek,* 29 September [Online]. Available at www.newsweek.com/2014/10/03/three-letter-word-driving-gender-revolution-272654.html (accessed 5 October 2015).
An interesting article about some kindergartens in Sweden that have started to use the word 'hen' to replace male and female pronouns.

Brooker, L. (2006) From home to the home corner: observing children's identity-maintenance in early childhood settings. *Children and Society,* 20: 116–127.
Can early years settings challenge stereotypes children may have picked up in their home environments or do they confirm them? This article argues that early years settings are ideally placed to encourage children to discuss their views on gender and ethnicity.

Cameron, C., Moss, P. and Owen, C. (1998) *Men as Workers in Services for Young Children: Issues of a Mixed Gender Workforce.* London: Institute of Education.
A very balanced and interesting overview of men in daycare – the benefits and the challenges.

Fine, C. (2010) *Delusions of Gender.* London: Icon Books.
This interesting book provides a clear and well-reasoned challenge to the argument that differences between male and female brains are the cause of gender inequalities.

Grabucker, M. (1988) *There's a Good Girl: Gender Stereotyping in the First Three Years – A Diary.* London: Women's Press.
A mother charts her attempts to raise her daughter in a gender neutral way. An updated version includes an afterword by the mother and the, now adult, daughter.

Hughes, S. (2015) Step aside, Barbie, this looks like a job for the new breed of girls' superhero action dolls. *The Guardian,* 10 October [Online]. Available at www.theguardian.com/lifeandstyle/2015/oct/10/super hero-girls-action-dolls-sexism-toy-industry-mattel (accessed 12 October 2015).
This is an article about a new range of superhero dolls that are all girls and there is no pink in sight! Acknowledging that girls want to experience feeling powerful, these dolls give girls the opportunity to join in an area of play that has generally been dominated by boys.

Keith, Lois (2001) *Take Up Thy Bed and Walk: Death, Disability and Cure in Classic Fiction for Girls.* London: Women's Press.
Very readable and interesting overview of how some of the classic 'books for girls' like *Little Women, Jane Eyre, Heidi* and *Pollyanna* all used images of death, disability and miraculous cures in order to 'punish' characters and redeem them through self-will.

LoBue, V. and DeLoache, J. (2011) Pretty in pink: the early development of gender-stereotyped colour preferences. *British Journal of Developmental Psychology,* 29: 656–667.
The results of a research study into the colour preferences of young children is discussed in this article with some interesting findings about girls and boys and pink and blue.

Zero Tolerance (2013) *Just Like a Child* [Online]. Available at www.dayprogramme.org/Challenging%20gender%20stereotyping.pdf (accessed 5 October 2015).
This is a very good resource that gives a clear outline explaining why this work with gender is so important. It also includes a range of practical ideas to use with resources to support their use. Highly recommended.

Index